RAND | NATIONAL SECURITY RESEARCH DIVISION

Getting Out from "In-Between"

Perspectives on the Regional Order in Post-Soviet Europe and Eurasia

Volume Editors: Samuel Charap, Alyssa Demus, Jeremy Shapiro

Contributing Authors: Samuel Charap, James Dobbins, Andrei Zagorski, Reinhard Krumm, Esther Ademmer, Yaroslav Lissovolik, Oleksandr Chalyi, Yulia Nikitina

For more information on this publication, visit www.rand.org/t/CF382

Library of Congress Cataloging-in-Publication Data is available for this publication.
ISBN: 978-1-9774-0033-8

Published by the RAND Corporation, Santa Monica, Calif.
© Copyright 2018 RAND Corporation
RAND® is a registered trademark.

Support RAND
Make a tax-deductible charitable contribution at
www.rand.org/giving/contribute

www.rand.org

Preface

Russia's relations with the West are in deep turmoil. This turmoil has manifested itself in various ways, including alleged Russian interference in U.S. and European elections, tit-for-tat diplomatic expulsions, and sanctions. These developments notwithstanding, the issue that originally sent the relationship off the rails and remains at the core of the broader dispute is the competition over Ukraine and Russia's other post-Soviet neighbors, the "in-between" states: Belarus, Moldova, Georgia, Armenia, and Azerbaijan. While the competitive dynamic between Russia and the West has come to a head in Ukraine, all of these states are objects of a contest among outside powers. This contest has become a negative-sum game, benefiting none of the parties: The West and Russia now find themselves locked into a dangerous and damaging competition as a result, while the states in the region remain to varying degrees unstable, unreformed, and rife with conflict.

With support from Carnegie Corporation of New York and the Swiss Federal Department of Foreign Affairs, and in partnership with the Regional Office for Cooperation and Peace in Europe of the Friedrich Ebert Stiftung, the RAND Corporation launched a study to explore alternatives to the current approaches to the regional order. A working group of experts and former policy practitioners from the United States, the European Union, Russia, and the in-between states met three times to explore possible common ground on the underlying principles of regional order. The papers which informed the group's discussions are presented in this volume. The challenge put to all the authors was to offer analysis and recommendations that help foster a regional architecture that is both appropriate for the particular circumstances of the in-between countries and acceptable to these countries, the West, and Russia.

This project was conducted within the International Security and Defense Policy Center (ISDP) of the RAND National Security Research Division (NSRD). NSRD conducts research and analysis on defense and national security topics for U.S. government agencies, private foundations, and the ministries of U.S. allies and partners.

For more information on the ISDP, see www.rand.org/nsrd/ndri/centers/isdp or contact the director (contact information is provided on the webpage).

Contents

Preface iii

Figures and Table vii

Contributor Biographies ix

Abbreviations xiii

CHAPTER ONE

Introduction
    Samuel Charap 1

CHAPTER TWO

Lessons Learned from Russia-West Interactions on European Security
    James Dobbins and Andrei Zagorski 5
A Complex History 5
Lessons to Learn 11
Conclusion 15

CHAPTER THREE

Small Steps: How to Start Improving Security in Europe
    Reinhard J. Krumm 17
The Evolution of Expectations 18
Trust and Distrust 20
Concrete Steps: Islands of Cooperation and Structured Dialogue 21

CHAPTER FOUR

Thoughts on Inclusive Economic Integration
    Esther Ademmer and Yaroslav Lissovolik 25
The Challenge of Inclusive Economic Integration 26
Ideas on How to Create Order 28

CHAPTER FIVE

Approaches to Resolving the Conflict over the States In Between
    Oleksandr Chalyi 33
Defining "In-Between" 33
The Case of Ukraine as an In-Between 34
Moving from Confrontation to Cooperation Regarding the States In Between 38

CHAPTER SIX

Cooperative Transregionalism and the Problem of the "In Betweens"
   Yulia Nikitina 41
Regional Integration as a Means to Prevent New Conflicts 41
Cooperative Transregionalism 43
Recommendations 45
Conclusions 47

CHAPTER SEVEN

Summary of Policy Recommendations 49

References 53

Figures and Table

Figures

1.1. The State of the Region 2

6.1. Model of Norm Diffusion Through Regional Integration 43

Table

6.1 The CSTO's Views on Areas of Possible Cooperation Between the CSTO and NATO 46

Contributor Biographies

The views expressed in this report are the chapter authors' alone and do not necessarily reflect those of the RAND Corporation.

Dr. Esther Ademmer is a post-doctoral researcher at the Kiel Institute for the World Economy and at Freie Universität Berlin, Germany. Her research interests include European integration and governance and the impact of external actors on the political economy of domestic change, especially in the post-Soviet space. Dr. Ademmer holds a doctorate in Political Science from Freie Universität and a Master of International Relations from Freie Universität/Humboldt-Universität zu Berlin and the University of Potsdam.

Ambassador Oleksandr Chalyi serves as the president of Grant Thornton, Ukraine, where he specializes in issues related to international and corporate law, particularly international agreements and contracts. Previously, he served as First Deputy Minister for Foreign Affairs of Ukraine, State Secretary for European Integration, and Foreign Policy Adviser to the President of Ukraine. He has headed Ukrainian delegations for World Trade Organization membership negotiations, with international institutions like the World Bank group, the European Bank for Reconstruction and Development, and the European Investment Bank. In 2014, he was named a member of the Organization for Security and Co-operation in Europe's Eminent Persons Panel.

Dr. Samuel Charap is a senior political scientist at the RAND Corporation. His work focuses on the political economy and foreign policies of Russia and the former Soviet states; European and Eurasian regional security; and U.S.-Russia deterrence, strategic stability, and arms control. From November 2012 until April 2017, Dr. Charap was the Senior Fellow for Russia and Eurasia at the International Institute for Strategic Studies. Prior to joining the International Institute for Strategic Studies, he served at the U.S. Department of State as Senior Adviser to the Undersecretary for Arms Control and International Security and on the secretary's Policy Planning Staff, covering Russia and Eurasia. He is the co-author, with Timothy Colton, of *Everyone Loses: The Ukraine Crisis and the Ruinous Contest for Post-Soviet Eurasia* (Routledge, 2017).

Alyssa Demus is a policy analyst at the RAND Corporation. Her work focuses on Central and Eastern European geopolitical issues, deterrence, influence and disinformation efforts, and other national security and defense issues. Prior to joining RAND, Ms. Demus served as a consultant to a variety of government and commercial clients, and conducted research examining various national and international security issues at a national security consulting firm. Ms. Demus also served as an Executive Fellow in the California Governor's Office Executive Fellowship program, working on issues related to homeland security and international agreements.

Ambassador James Dobbins is a senior fellow and Distinguished Chair in Diplomacy and Security at the RAND Corporation. He has held State Department and White House posts, including Assistant Secretary of State for Europe, Special Assistant to the President for the Western Hemisphere, Special Adviser to the President, Secretary of State for the Balkans, and Ambassador to the European Community. Ambassador Dobbins has served on numerous crisis management and diplomatic troubleshooting assignments as special envoy for Afghanistan and Pakistan, Kosovo, Bosnia, Haiti, and Somalia for the administrations of Barack Obama, George W. Bush, and Bill Clinton. In 2013, he returned to the State Department to become the Obama administration's Special Representative for Afghanistan and Pakistan, returning to RAND in 2014.

Dr. Reinhard Krumm heads the newly established Regional Office for Cooperation and Peace in Europe of the Friedrich Ebert Stiftung. He holds a doctorate from Regensburg University, Germany, where he has been a lecturer on Russian history since 2008. From 1991 to 1998, he was a journalist in the former Soviet Union, working as the Moscow correspondent of *Der Spiegel* from 1996 to 1998. He joined the Friedrich Ebert Stiftung in 2002, serving as the head of the Regional Central Asian office in Tashkent, Uzbekistan from 2003 to 2007, the head of the Russian office in Moscow from 2007 to 2012, and the head of the Department of Central and Eastern Europe in Berlin from 2012 to 2016.

Dr. Yaroslav Lissovolik is the chief economist at the Eurasian Development Bank. He worked at the International Monetary Fund in Washington in 2001–2004, where he was Adviser to the Executive Director for the Russian Federation. Dr. Lissovolik is a member of the Scientific and Methodological Council of the Federal State Statistics Service, a member of the Council on Foreign and Defense policy, and a member of the Bretton Woods Committee. He became a member of the Expert Council of the Russian government in 2012, as well as of the Working Group on macroeconomic policy of the Presidential Economic Council. Dr. Lissovolik became the Program Director of the Valdai International Discussion Club in 2016. He has published books on Russia's entry to the World Trade Organization and on Russia's integration into the world economy, as well as numerous articles and papers on economic and policy issues.

Dr. Yulia Nikitina is associate professor of World Politics and Research Fellow at the Center for Post-Soviet Studies at Moscow State Institute of International Relations. She is a specialist on security in Eurasia with a focus on regional organizations. She is the author of the Russian-language book *The CSTO and SCO: Models of Security Regionalism (2009) and of the textbook Introduction to World Politics and International Relations* (2009).

Jeremy Shapiro is research director at the European Council on Foreign Relations. Previously he was a fellow in the Project on International Order and Strategy and the Center on the United States and Europe at the Brookings Institution, where he edited the Foreign Policy program's blog *Order from Chaos*. Prior to Brookings, Mr. Shapiro was a member of the U.S. State Department's policy planning staff, where he advised the Secretary of State on U.S. policy in

North Africa and the Levant. Mr. Shapiro was also the senior adviser to Assistant Secretary of State for European and Eurasian Affairs Philip Gordon, providing strategic guidance on a wide variety of U.S.-European foreign policy issues.

Dr. Andrei Zagorski is the director of the Department of Arms Control and Conflict Resolution Studies at the Primakov Institute of World Economy and International Relations of the Russian Academy of Sciences, and Professor of International Relations at the Moscow State Institute of International Relations. Dr. Zagorski's work focuses on European security, relations between Russia and NATO, and relations between Russian and European organizations (Organization for Security and Co-operation in Europe, the European Union, European Council). From 1981 to 1992, he was a full-time researcher at the Center for International Studies of the Moscow State Institute of International Relations. From 1992 to 1999, he was a Vice-Rector of the Moscow State Institute of International Relations. From 1999 to 2000, he was a Senior Vice President of the EastWest Institute, in Prague. In 2001, he served as director of the project "Networking of the Early Warning Systems" of the EastWest Institute. He has held his current position since 2011.

Abbreviations

A/CFE	Adapted Treaty on Conventional Forces in Europe
AA	Association Agreement
ASEAN	Association of Southeast Asian Nations
BRI	China's Belt and Road Initiative
CFE	Treaty on Conventional Forces in Europe
CIS	Commonwealth of Independent States
CSBM	confidence and security-building measure
CSCE	Conference on Security and Cooperation in Europe
CSTO	Collective Security Treaty Organization
DCFTA	Deep and Comprehensive Free Trade Area agreement
EAEU	Eurasian Economic Union
EaP	Eastern Partnership
EBRD	European Bank for Reconstruction and Development
ECE	East Central European
EDB	Eurasian Development Bank
EFTA	European Free Trade Association
EU	European Union
FTA	free trade agreement
MAP	Membership Action Plan
NATO	North Atlantic Treaty Organization
NPT	Nuclear Non-Proliferation Treaty
NTB	nontariff barrier

OSCE	Organization for Security and Co-operation in Europe
SCO	Shanghai Cooperation Organization
UN	United Nations
WTO	World Trade Organization

CHAPTER ONE

Introduction

Samuel Charap, Ph.D.
Senior Political Scientist
RAND Corporation

At the core of the dispute between Russia and the West is the contest over the countries physi-cally located between them: Ukraine first and foremost, but also Belarus, Moldova, Georgia, Armenia, and Azerbaijan. While the relationship between Russia and the West was far from ideal before 2014, it was the Ukraine crisis, particularly Moscow's annexation of Crimea and invasion of eastern Ukraine, that fundamentally changed that relationship, ruling out any remaining hopes for partnership and effectively institutionalizing a confrontational dynamic. The contest over the "in-between" states (Figure 1.1) has taken a significant toll on these states themselves. The most extreme case is the war in Ukraine, in which over 10,000 have died; other regional conflicts have occurred in Moldova, Georgia and Azerbaijan, and the competi-tion has also disrupted regional trade patterns and set back the process of reform and domestic transformation in these states. The status quo is thus far from optimal for all parties.

Western policy debates regarding the future of the regional order are usually between advocates of further enlargement of Euro-Atlantic institutions, and their critics, who argue that enlargement caused the current crisis and should be called to a halt. This debate is increas-ingly divorced from the realities on the ground in Europe and Eurasia: a European Union (EU) engulfed in a multifaceted crisis; a United States looking to reduce commitments in Europe; an absence of political will in either the EU or the North Atlantic Treaty Organization (NATO) to offer full membership to the in-between states; in-between states that are in no condition to qualify for membership; and ongoing conflicts in the three most plausible mem-bership aspirants, including a major war in Ukraine. However, the critics of enlargement offer no compelling alternative vision for regional integration, which makes their position unten-able. Russia, too, does not seem to have viable solutions at hand; its integration offerings are largely unappealing to elites in the in-between countries, so much so that it has had to resort to armed coercion in order to pursue its interests.

In short, both Russian and Western policy toward these states has seemingly reached a dead end. Continuing with the status quo will perpetuate instability and poor governance in the states of the region and a long-term Cold War-like atmosphere in West-Russia relations. But without an intellectually credible alternative to the status quo, both the West and Russia seemed doomed to continue it.

The RAND Corporation convened a distinguished group of scholars and former prac-titioners from the in-between states, the United States, Russia, and the EU to explore the

Figure 1.1
The State of the Region

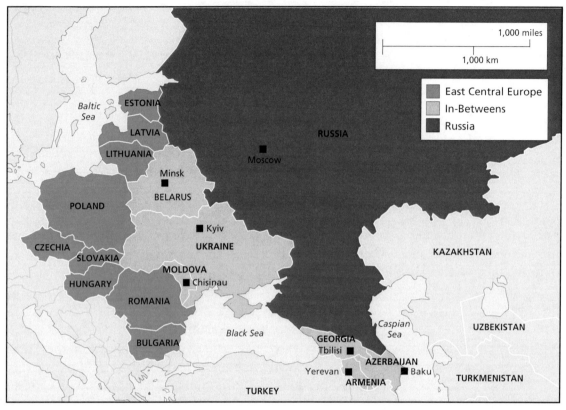

outlines of such a credible alternative. The group, which, in addition to the authors, included Jeremy Shapiro, Adam Kobieracki, Syuzanna Vasilyan, and Michael Leigh, met three times and discussed the issues at the core of the dispute over the regional order. These discussions, while conducted on a not-for-attribution basis, were informed by the papers presented in this volume. While we have edited the papers for style and language, the analyses presented are those of the respective authors. The papers and discussion are among the first attempts to present alternative frameworks for regional order that could mitigate the current crisis.

James Dobbins and Andrei Zagorski offer a unique perspective on lessons learned from post–Cold War Russia-West interactions regarding the regional order. They argue that the first enlargements of NATO and the EU actually followed a very different pattern from what occurred after 2004. Before then, the West made a strong effort to keep a parallel track of engagement with Russia as it enlarged Euro-Atlantic institutions. With the EU's Eastern Partnership (EaP) and the push for a Membership Action Plan (MAP) for Georgia and Ukraine at the 2008 NATO Bucharest summit, however, engagement with Russia was disregarded. Russia's concerns were no longer being addressed, they argue, "in a cooperative manner . . . In this environment, an increasingly assertive Moscow demonstrated its readiness and ability to resist further erosion of the status quo in its immediate geopolitical environs." Based on their review of this history, they offer a number of innovative, concrete proposals to de-escalate the present conflict, including multilateral security guarantees, new arms control provisions, and a recommitment to nonintervention.

In his piece, Reinhard Krumm argues that rather than viewing trust as a precondition for cooperation, "small steps" toward what he calls "islands of cooperation," such as the recent Russia-Georgia trade talks or Organization for Security and Co-operation in Europe (OSCE) structured dialogue processes, present the most promising path forward.

In their contribution, Esther Ademmer and Yaroslav Lissovolik examine the challenges for inclusive economic integration in the region. They note that economic relations are not the source of the conflict over the regional order, but economic links have been a casualty of the conflict as technocratic matters of trade policy have become highly politicized. They propose a number of steps that could address the current situation, including bilateral agreements among regional states and trade blocs where none exist today, and an inclusive dialogue among the commissions of the EU, the Eurasian Economic Union (EAEU), and states that do not belong to either group.

Oleksandr Chalyi's paper looks at three interrelated subjects. First, he begins with a critical examination of what it means to be an "in-between" state. He notes that Armenia and Belarus are not truly in between, as they have joined the EAEU and the Collective Security Treaty Organization (CSTO). Including them in the same basket as Ukraine would mean we must include countries that belong to NATO and the EU as well. Second, based on his personal experience as a decisionmaker in Ukraine, he offers three scenarios for Ukraine's future, the best of which, "Cold Peace," would nonetheless require a transformation of the Russia-West dynamic from confrontation to cooperation. The last section of his chapter offers recommendations on how to achieve that transformation, with targeted suggestions for the great powers, the in-between states, and regional organizations.

Yulia Nikitina examines the role of regional institutions in Russia-West disputes over the regional order. She notes that Russia and the West have different conceptions of the purpose and role of regional institutions. Nikitina appraises several alternative frameworks aimed at fostering cooperation between Russia-led and Euro-Atlantic regional institutions. She concludes with recommendations, which include ideas for an agenda for discussions between NATO and the CSTO, such as postconflict reconstruction in Syria.

We are grateful to Carnegie Corporation of New York and the Swiss Federal Department of Foreign Affairs for their generous support of this effort and to the Friedrich Ebert Stiftung for its partnership in conducting the project.

CHAPTER TWO

Lessons Learned from Russia-West Interactions on European Security

Ambassador James Dobbins
Senior Fellow, Distinguished Chair in Diplomacy and Security
RAND Corporation

Andrei Zagorski, Ph.D.
Director of the Department of Arms Control and Conflict Resolution Studies
Primakov Institute of World Economy and International Relations, Russian Academy of Sciences

Throughout the Cold War, Europe was divided into two military and economic blocs, with only a few small countries left in between. Sweden, Finland, Austria, and Switzerland were free-market democracies that maintained their neutrality and were part of the European Free Trade Association (EFTA). Yugoslavia and Albania were communist states that did not join, or in the case of Albania, left the Soviet-dominated Warsaw Pact alliance. With the end of the Cold War, this order was upended. Germany's reunification, the dissolution of the Warsaw Pact, and the collapse of the Soviet Union left the countries of the former Eastern bloc adrift, without multilateral trade or security links, while also freeing the formerly neutral nations from the conflicting pressures imposed by East-West competition.

This paper provides a shared Russian and American perspective on the manner in which the European institutional architecture has developed since then, the problems these developments pose, and some recommendations for deescalating the resulting confrontation between Russia and the West.

A Complex History

The End of the Cold War

At the end of the Cold War, the eastward enlargement of NATO was not a subject for consideration. Rather, the single issue concerning both the Soviet Union and the West was the status of a unified Germany. Western representatives assured their Soviet interlocutors that they had no intention of extending NATO eastward.[1] These assurances were never formalized or made

---

[1] See Maxim Korshunov, "Mikhail Gorbachev: I Am Against All Walls," *Russia Beyond the Headlines*, October 16, 2014; see also a speech by the Soviet ambassador to West Germany at the time of reunification, Vladislav Terekhov, "Ob'edinenie Germanii i problema rasshireniya NATO: chto obeshchal Zapad?" Moscow State Institute of International Relations, December 21, 2009. Scholarly literature covering this issue includes Mary Elise Sarotte, "Not One Inch Eastward? Bush, Baker, Kohl, Genscher, Gorbachev, and the Origin of Russian Resentment Toward NATO Enlargement in February 1990,"

more precise. At the time of German reunification, the Warsaw Pact remained in effect, and Washington was not encouraging defections. Had Moscow insisted on formal agreements limiting NATO's further enlargement as a condition for Soviet withdrawal from East Germany, the West German government would likely have agreed, as would have the United States. However, the Soviet leadership did not make such a demand; instead, it agreed to allowing a unified Germany into NATO. The sides did negotiate a special regime for the territory of the former East Germany: combat forces of NATO countries—particularly the United States—would not be permanently deployed in the eastern part of the country, while German territorial defense forces and temporary deployments, e.g. for the purpose of exercises, were allowed.

In this same period immediately following the end of the Cold War, the term "Euro-Atlantic" was first employed to denote a community wider than the Atlantic community (i.e., NATO) or the European Community—it referred to a community in which the Soviet Union would be a full member. The use of this phrase not only signified a change in rhetoric, but also in practice. For instance, by 1994, the Conference on Security and Cooperation in Europe (CSCE) had been transformed into the OSCE and gained permanent institutions, including a secretariat, a conflict prevention center, an office for democratic institutions and human rights, a high commissioner for national minorities, and a parliamentary assembly. Also at this time, Moscow and Washington discussed prospects for a transformation of NATO and the Warsaw Pact toward their politicization. Within a new inclusive post–Cold War European order, many hoped that alliances eventually could be transcended by growing cooperation on the platform of the institutionalized OSCE. The 1990 Charter of Paris and declarations made at subsequent CSCE/OSCE meetings during the 1990s kept this option open.[2]

The dismantlement of the Cold War order was accompanied by intense communication, openness, and mutual respect among the former adversaries, with NATO members demonstrating readiness to cooperatively and constructively address concerns raised by Moscow. None of the concepts floated at the time excluded the Soviet Union/Russia from an extended Euro-Atlantic community. Russia itself embarked on a path of transformation compatible with the trajectory of the post-communist transformation of the East Central European (ECE) countries.

The First NATO/EU Enlargements

With the dissolution of the Warsaw Pact and the collapse of the Soviet Union, the status of former Warsaw Pact member states was indeterminate. What would be their ongoing economic and security relationship with Russia on the one hand and with NATO and the European Community on the other? It was unclear whether these states might choose neutrality and seek to join the EFTA or swing all the way toward pursuing NATO and EU membership.

By the mid-1990s, the question was decided: Russia was confronted with the prospect of an institutional extension of the EU and NATO into the ECE region. The geographic scope of eventual enlargements was unclear at the time, but, by 1997, a total of 12 countries, includ-

Diplomatic History, Vol. 34, No. 1, 2010, pp. 119–140, and Mary Elise Sarotte, "Perpetuating U.S. Preeminence: The 1990 Deals to 'Bribe the Soviets Out' and Move NATO in," *International Security*, Vol. 35, No. 1, 2010, pp. 110–113.

2   See OSCE, Charter of Paris for a New Europe, Paris, November 21, 1990. For an overview of the debates and references to relevant OSCE documents see Andrei Zagorski, "The Transformation of Russia-ECE Relations," in Andrei Zagorski, ed., *Russia and East Central Europe After the Cold War: A Fundamentally Transformed Relationship*, Prague: Human Rights Publishers, 2015, pp. 26–58.

ing the Baltic states, had applied for NATO membership. These same states also sought membership in the EU. The positions of the three Westernmost ECE states—Poland, the Czech Republic, and Hungary—became clear first. They pressed for NATO and EU membership. After some debate, these Western institutions responded positively.

In these initial post–Cold War years, while Russia preferred that the OSCE play a central role in the emerging European security architecture, Moscow did not react strongly to the initial eastward extension of the West, provided its interests were taken into account. From 1996, Russia and the leading Western countries engaged in intense dialogue on the terms of the enlargement. Apart from specific security-related concerns, Russia raised broader issues with a view to achieving a respectful Russian integration with the expanding Western community.

On the Western side, the NATO enlargement decision was the product of divergent views on Russia. The former Warsaw Pact countries feared a revanchist Russia and sought protection. Most Western governments no longer feared post-Soviet Russia and therefore saw little cost or risk in taking on these new defense commitments; they also believed that the incentives created by the membership process would spur reform. In the economic sphere, it was clear that the EU had more to offer the ECE than did Russia, which was in the midst of its post-Soviet economic turmoil, and it was equally clear that it would be much easier for the EU to absorb the smaller ECE states than to absorb Russia. Rather than craft new arrangements applicable to the entire former Eastern bloc, as had been discussed in the late 1980s and early 1990s, both NATO and the EU chose to pursue a differentiated approach that distinguished between Russia and the other Warsaw Pact states.

In response, and largely at the expense of the pan-European OSCE, Moscow sought to institutionalize bilateral relations with NATO and the EU in a way that would give it some association with both organizations that fell short of membership. Future institutions were intended to provide a platform for regular political consultations, joint decisionmaking and, eventually, joint action, as well as a platform where Russian concerns would be heard and addressed in a cooperative manner.

Specifically, Moscow sought to curb increases in NATO's military capabilities, particularly the deployment of combat forces and nuclear assets in the ECE countries. It also wanted to establish a geographic limit to any *further* NATO eastward extension. Initially, it sought to prevent membership of the Baltic states by negotiating a "red line" that NATO would not cross.

As a result of intense communications with the West, Russia got almost all of what it was asking for. In 1994, Russia and NATO settled on a modest agreement that established a mechanism for enhanced political dialogue.[3] The 1997 NATO-Russia Founding Act then upgraded and further institutionalized this interaction.[4] In that document, NATO committed itself, *inter alia*, to refrain from additional permanent deployments of substantial combat forces and stated that it did not intend to deploy nuclear weapons in new locations on the continent. In 1999, the Adapted Treaty on Conventional Forces in Europe (A/CFE) was signed, which updated the original 1990 treaty in large part to address Russian concerns about that document. Yet none of these agreements instituted Russia's desired "red line" for NATO enlarge-

---

[3] NATO, Areas for Pursuance of a Broad, Enhanced NATO/Russia Dialogue and Cooperation, Noordwijk, May 31, 1995.

[4] NATO, Founding Act on Mutual Relations, Cooperation and Security Between NATO and the Russian Federation, Paris, May 27, 1997.

ment. While addressing many Russian concerns, the West carefully avoided any agreement that would give Moscow a *droit de regard* over its future decisions.

The 2004 NATO enlargement incorporated the three Baltic states—Estonia, Latvia, and Lithuania—which had been integral parts of the Soviet Union. A similar dynamic was in play as during the first round: The Baltic states sought protection from Russia, while the Western powers were focused on fostering the transition from communism and did not consider Russia a serious security threat. The near impossibility of actually defending these states was never a serious consideration; if it had been, it is fair to say that their NATO membership would not have been likely.

The three Baltic states came into NATO largely on the coattails of the three new Balkan members (Slovenia, Bulgaria and Romania). The conflict in the former Yugoslavia persuaded Western capitals that the Balkan states needed to be offered the prospect of NATO and EU membership to help stem the region's ethnic, religious, and nationalist tensions. However, the U.S. public was much more sympathetic toward the accession of the three Baltic states—the incorporation of which into the Soviet Union the United States had never recognized—than toward Slovenia, Bulgaria or Romania. Thus, the inclusion of the Baltic states in the second wave of NATO expansion was the price necessary to secure its ratification by the U.S. Senate.[5]

For Russia, the most controversial issue was the membership of the Baltic states. There was a clear understanding between Russia and NATO that the 2004 enlargement was accompanied by a new arrangement between them. Indeed, as in the 1997 Founding Act's signing in the run-up to the 1999 enlargement, the formal invitation of new countries to join the alliance was preceded in 2002 by the signing of the NATO-Russia Rome Declaration, which further transformed the NATO-Russia Council.[6]

The cooperative and consultative nature of discussions over NATO and EU enlargement up through 2004 signaled to Moscow that the West sincerely honored the OSCE commitment to consider other states' legitimate security concerns while exercising "the right to belong or not to belong to international organizations, to be or not to be a party to bilateral or multilateral treaties, including treaties of alliance."[7]

In short, the NATO-Russia relationship was certainly not uncontroversial in the 15 years following the Cold War, but Moscow had a sense that its concerns were heard and addressed in a cooperative way. Although it did so without enthusiasm, it accepted and respected the accession of these additional ECE European countries to both NATO and the EU. Moscow expected that the other Soviet successor states would remain in its orbit, assuming that the Baltic states represented a special case. Although there was no explicit or tacit agreement to this effect, the West had not yet seriously challenged this Russian ambition. After the 2004 eastward enlargement, Moscow's expectation was that further eastward expansion of the West would halt, at least for a time, leaving Russia time to consolidate a new status quo, not least by pursuing various integration initiatives with and among its immediate neighbors.

---

[5] James Dobbins, *Foreign Service: Five Decades on the Frontlines of American Diplomacy*, Washington, D.C.: Brookings Institution Press, 2017, p. 229.

[6] NATO, NATO-Russia Relations: A New Quality: Declaration by Heads of State and Government of NATO Member States and the Russian Federation, Rome, May 28, 2002.

[7] OSCE, Code of Conduct on Politico-Military Aspects of Security, Budapest, December 3, 1994.

Relations Deteriorate, Pressure on the In-Betweens Intensifies

However, troubles began with the so-called "color revolutions" in several former-Soviet states, in Georgia in 2003, Ukraine in 2004–2005, and Kyrgyzstan in 2005. Russia saw these uprisings as a manifestation of a Western—largely U.S.—regime change policy. This policy, from Russia's perspective, was aimed at installing pro-Western governments, reducing the influence of Russia in the region and perhaps even, one day, promoting regime change in Russia itself. Soon thereafter, NATO and EU enlargement into the former Soviet region reappeared on the Western agenda. This was manifest in the discussion of NATO MAPs for Georgia and Ukraine at the April 2008 NATO Bucharest summit. At this summit, France and Germany resisted then–U.S. President George W. Bush's push to offer MAPs to Ukraine and Georgia, but they agreed to issue a statement declaring flatly that "we agree today that these countries will become members of NATO," despite the fact that most Ukrainians at the time did not want to do so.[8]

With the launch of the EU's EaP in 2009, which offered the countries "in between" (Moldova, Ukraine, Belarus, Georgia, Armenia, and Azerbaijan) political association and economic integration with the EU, though not full membership, the EU became a major revisionist actor alongside the United States in Moscow's eyes. As distinct from the 1990s, the West's policy toward the former Soviet states was no longer pursued in consultation with Russia. In fact, the Bush administration pursued NATO MAPs knowing full well that Russia vehemently objected. And compared to the intensive and largely constructive communication between Moscow and Brussels in the late 1990s regarding enlargement, Russia and the EU never formally discussed the eventual and perceived consequences of the implementation of the EU's EaP policy. Additionally, the EU did not make any attempts to cooperatively address related Russian concerns. As a result, for many in the West, all of Europe became conceptually divided into three categories—NATO/EU members, prospective NATO/EU members, and Russia.

In this new environment, disagreement on relatively peripheral issues often would trigger a chain reaction and lead to significant unintended consequences, threatening the cooperative regimes established at the end of the Cold War, which were considered in both Russia and the West as cornerstones of European security. For example, at the end of 2003, the "Kozak Memorandum"—a settlement brokered by a special envoy of President Vladimir Putin between the Moldovan president and the leadership of breakaway Transnistria—was torpedoed by the intervention of the United States and the EU. Moscow responded by terminating the withdrawal and the disposal of a Soviet-era arms and munition dump in Transnistria. Given that Russian withdrawal from Moldova was linked to ratification of A/CFE by NATO member states, the new treaty never entered into force.

In 2007, as a result of this development Moscow "suspended" implementation of the original Treaty on Conventional Forces in Europe (CFE) and declared that it did so in hopes of spurring NATO's ratification of A/CFE. However, while the Russian goal may have been to persuade NATO member-states to ratify A/CFE, it failed to achieve it. Meanwhile, the West failed in its goal of ensuring Russian withdrawal from Moldova. After a series of attempts to save and revive the CFE regime, this sequence of events resulted in an almost complete collapse of conventional arms control and of cooperative security in Europe.

---

[8] NATO, Bucharest Summit Declaration, Bucharest, April 3, 2008; Kathleen Holzwart Sprehe, "Ukraine Says 'No' to NATO," Pew Research Center, March 29, 2010.

Over these same years, the trajectory of Russia's domestic transformation and foreign policy changed. After having briefly considered NATO and EU membership at the beginning of Putin's first term in the office, Moscow dropped the idea and no longer sought any sort of integration with the West. The perception of ongoing global redistribution of economic power toward "non-Western" nations contributed to the weakening appeal of the liberal-democratic and competitive market model within Russia.

Having dropped the idea of any sort of institutional membership in the West, Moscow embarked on the path of consolidating multilateral frameworks within the post-Soviet space, seeing this as a single way to prevent its further penetration by the West. This policy accelerated in 2009 with the creation of the Eurasian Customs Union, which later became the EAEU. Together with the CSTO, the two institutions were intended to form a Eurasian community of states—a purported alternative to the Euro-Atlantic community.

Conflicts Intensify

The same 2008 NATO Bucharest declaration that expressed the conviction that Ukraine and Georgia would one day become members went on to state that the accession of new members to NATO would "bring us closer to our goal of a Europe that is whole, free, and at peace."[9] In practice, the effect was quite the opposite. Four months after the Bucharest meeting, a brief conflict broke out between Russia and Georgia, after which Russia recognized the independence of two breakaway regions of Georgia (Abkhazia and South Ossetia). Six years later, Russia annexed Crimea and supported the insurgency in the Donbas. The proximate cause of these latter actions was the overthrow of the government of Ukrainian President Viktor Yanukovych. This revolt was prompted by Yanukovych's decision to postpone the signing of an Association Agreement (AA) with the EU, which included a Deep and Comprehensive Free Trade Area agreement (DCFTA) at its core, in favor of closer cooperation with Russia short actually of seeking membership in the EAEU. While the EU AA was not necessarily a step toward membership, the agreement, and particularly the DCFTA, was designed to align the Ukrainian economy and society more closely with EU norms. Ukraine's signing of the agreement would have made the country's membership in the EAEU impossible, thus presenting Ukraine with a binary choice between the two blocs.

These frozen or, in the case of the Donbas, still-active conflicts effectively block any moves toward NATO membership for either Georgia or Ukraine. They also make it even less likely that Russia could ever be incorporated in any Euro-Atlantic collective security arrangement, given the heightened fear of Russia among its immediate neighbors engendered by these actions. As a result, NATO has once again become a defensive alliance directed primarily at Russia.

Russia, meanwhile, seeks to delineate geographic areas of responsibility between the Euro-Atlantic and the Eurasian communities. This would entail institutionalizing relations between NATO and the CSTO, as well as between the EU and the EAEU. Washington and other Western governments continue to reject any arrangement based upon such implicit spheres of influence, insisting that the in-between states have the right to choose their alignments, even if Western organizations are not ready to accept them as members any time soon.

---

[9]   NATO, 2008.

These developments posed a dilemma to the countries in between that were not members of either the EAEU/CSTO or the EU/NATO. They were increasingly confronted with difficult either-or decisions, culminating in 2013 when they had to make a choice between signing or not signing AAs with the EU. While Georgia, Moldova and Ukraine opted for AAs, Armenia joined the EAEU. These choices remain controversial within some of those countries. Of course, there was a third alternative—to seek no close association with either community of states—a policy that has been pursued by one country "in between," Azerbaijan, which has instead joined the nonaligned movement. It did not seek an AA with the EU, while showing no interest in either the CSTO, the EAEU, or even the free trade arrangement within the Commonwealth of Independent States (CIS).

Lessons to Learn

The landscape for the in-between states and for Russia has significantly changed as compared to the late 1990s and the early 2000s, when NATO and the EU went through their major eastward enlargement. As a result, the in-between states have increasingly become hostage to disputes between Russia and the West.

In that earlier period, the eastward enlargement of the Euro-Atlantic community was limited to the ECE region and did not include parts of the former Soviet Union, except for the Baltic states, which were seen as a special case. Furthermore, the West did not seriously challenge either the economic integration or the security role of Russia in the former Soviet region and was open to cooperatively addressing concerns raised by Russia in the context of NATO and EU enlargement. Although Moscow was not given veto power on decisions concerning the status of the countries concerned, it was part of the relevant mechanisms for joint decisionmaking with the United States and the West and engaged in intensive communication concerning the enlargements. At that time, the overall vector of Russian policy was based on the desire to foster a close partnership with the West presupposing a community of shared liberal values.

By contrast, the increasing tensions over the past decade have developed in a very different environment. The non-Baltic former Soviet states became the focal point of the competition between Russia and the West. Not only the NATO open door policy, but also the EU's EaP policy, were increasingly seen in Moscow as challenging the status quo in Russia's backyard. At the same time, Russia's involvement in common decisionmaking with the United States has been reduced to votes on the United Nations (UN) Security Council, which Washington sometimes felt it could ignore, and the OSCE, which had been marginalized by previous enlargements of NATO and the EU. Thus, in Moscow's view, concerns that had accumulated over the last decade were no longer addressed appropriately and in a cooperative manner. In this environment, an increasingly assertive Moscow demonstrated its readiness and ability to resist further erosion of the status quo in its immediate geopolitical environs.

Options for De-escalation

Based on this review of recent history, it becomes clear that seeking de-escalation between Russia and the West regarding the contested status of the countries in between would require facing certain realities. First, Russia is unlikely to change its domestic development or foreign policy radically, particularly in regard to its immediate neighborhood, in at least the short to midterm. Second, it is unlikely that definitive solutions regarding the final geopolitical orientation of the countries in between will be found soon. Although sweeping changes may be unlikely, both sides could undertake efforts to make the problem less acute, immediate, and urgent by creating mechanisms that would make it easier for all the involved parties to tolerate the current uncertainties and ambiguities over an extended period. Finally, it needs to be acknowledged that without an arrangement between Russia and the West to mitigate and manage their disagreement, the countries in between will hardly feel secure as long as their status is subject to this dispute.

The tensions and open conflicts that have resulted from Moscow's resistance to NATO and EU enlargement into the former-Soviet region might be addressed by a definitive halt to those processes. This might take the form of formal NATO and EU decision to declare limits to future enlargement that would exclude further former-Soviet states. In exchange Russia might be expected to end the region's frozen conflicts on terms acceptable to the affected states. Though it seems unlikely that Crimea would be returned to Ukraine, Russia might be expected, as part of such an arrangement, to join in settlements that result in the removal of its forces from the Donbas, Transnistria, South Ossetia, and Abkhazia. These forces would be replaced, where necessary, by genuinely international peacekeepers. Moscow and Brussels would also need to work out arrangements to maximize the benefits the affected states could derive from relations with the EU and the EAEU without requiring full membership in either customs union.

Such an agreement would require that the United States and Russia as well as NATO and EU member states all explicitly renounce long-espoused principles, promises, and policies. This seems unlikely on all sides. While Russia would welcome guarantees from NATO and the EU clearly delineating the ultimate final geographic reach of these organizations, it is unlikely that Moscow would be ready to pay the price by withdrawing its forces from Transnistria, the Donbas, and particularly Abkhazia and South Ossetia. Likewise, NATO and the EU would likely find it impossible to reach consensus on renouncing the open-door policy.

A second, messier but more-attainable alternative could be a series of understandings and agreements involving most (if not all) OSCE members. These understandings and agreements would push any changes in the alignment of the former-Soviet states into the distant future while creating a more favorable economic and security environment for these countries in the interim. Ultimately, such a set of arrangements should seek to reduce the pressures on the in-between states to seek membership in political-military alliances and, possibly, to make such membership unnecessary by increasing the benefits and incentives to pursue policies of non-alignment. This should not, however, prevent their closer economic integration and/or cooperation with both the EU or Russia/EAEU.

Such understandings between East and West would probably need to be accompanied by a series of broader agreements involving all of the Euro-Atlantic states designed to allow the states in between to develop, prosper, and remain independent, much as the neutral states of Europe did during the Cold War.

Such an arrangement may not be inconsistent with the current unstated and unacknowledged de facto policy of NATO, which, on the one hand, maintains its open door-policy but, on the other, has shelved the issue of eventual membership of Ukraine and is not pushing for a MAP for Georgia, let alone membership. Nor would it be inconsistent with the current policy of the EU since membership in the EU was never an objective of the EaP policy, and is unlikely to appear on the agenda anytime soon. This does not provide Russia with any guarantees that the countries in between would never again seek membership in Western institutions, but it would move that possibility into a more distant future and begin to create incentives for the in-between states to accept the status quo.

Such arrangements and understandings would require components addressing issues such as credible security guarantees to nonaligned countries; a set of measures, including arms control measures, to support such guarantees; an arrangement to make in-between states' association with the EU compatible with normalized economic ties with Russia and the EAEU; and a mutual commitment to engage in political consultations should the question of the status of the in-between states arise at any time in the future.

Multilateral Security Guarantees

The failure of the 1994 Budapest Memorandum, which was supposed to provide security assurances to Ukraine, has significantly undermined the credibility of such non-legally binding assurances from Russia and the West that could be given to the countries in between. Endorsing such guarantees by a UN Security Council resolution would make them legally binding. Regardless, concerns over the credibility of such promises are likely to remain for some time. In order to make multilateral security guarantees more credible and attractive to nonaligned countries, they should be supported by relevant and verifiable arms control arrangements.

The Benefits and Promises of the Nonaligned Status

Ukraine and the other in-between states could be offered, as a component of these arrangements, reliable assurances that their territory will not be used as a theater of hostilities between Russia and the West. The countries in between would also likely require guarantees that they would not be pushed into Russia's orbit against their wishes.

In return, the relevant countries would need to pledge not to allow any permanent deployments of foreign combat forces or use of military infrastructure on their territory. They would also need to guarantee that their territory would not be used for intelligence gathering or other hostile activities targeting any of the countries that have provided them with security guarantees.

In this scenario, the countries that have offered multilateral security guarantees to the in-betweens would need to vow to refrain from deploying combat forces on the territory of the latter.[10] Likewise, they would have to pledge not to use the in-betweens' territory for intelligence gathering or other hostile activities aimed against other parties that have joined the multilateral security guarantees. These commitments should not foreclose temporary deployments such as those involved in joint exercises or training, assuming that these activities would be subject to relevant transparency measures for all signatories of the multilateral security guarantees.

The proposed arrangement should establish both bilateral and multilateral cooperative mechanisms that allow the in-between states, as well as other parties to the multilateral security guarantees, to cooperatively address any concerns about compliance with the agreements.

Under any such agreement, Russia would need to withdraw its forces from the Donbas region of Ukraine. The parties would need to agree to disagree about the status of Crimea, Abkhazia, and South Ossetia, and to isolate, as best they can, those disagreements from other elements of interaction, such as the United States and Soviet Union did in regard to the status of the Baltic states. In any case, U.S. and EU sanctions linked to those disputes would remain, as would Ukrainian and Georgian claims to these territories.

---

[10] Special provisions would have to be made for territories that remain disputed, such as Crimea.

Arms Control Measures

Any multilateral security guarantees should be supported and substantiated by a verifiable agreement committing all parties not to concentrate substantial combat forces on the borders of neutral or nonaligned states (the width of this effectively demilitarized area would be subject to negotiation) and not to conduct large-scale military exercises there. Any military activities of the parties below the level of large-scale exercises (as defined in the agreement) should be conducted in a transparent, verifiable, and cooperative manner. Parties should avoid threatening scenarios for such exercises that could raise concerns in the countries in between.

Nonintervention in Internal Affairs

In order to address concerns pertaining to activities associated with hybrid conflict (measures short of conventional military hostilities), nonaligned countries in between should also receive assurances of nonintervention into their internal affairs. The OSCE could be an appropriate institution to address this issue in a cooperative manner. It could do so by further elaborating on the commitments of its participating states with respect to the already accepted principle of nonintervention in internal affairs. It could further consider establishing a cooperative mechanism that would allow states to bring concerns pertaining to alleged cases of interference in their domestic affairs to the attention of the organization. For this purpose, the OSCE could set up a commission to examine such allegations.[11] The relevant provisions of the 1970 UN Declaration on Principles of International Law concerning Friendly Relations and Cooperation among States in Accordance with the Charter of the United Nations can serve as the point of departure for this endeavor.[12]

Making EU DCFTAs and Economic Ties with the EAEU Compatible

A number of the countries in between have already concluded AA/DCFTAs with the EU or joined the EAEU. Russia, the EU and the countries in between would have to agree on terms to make the EU DCFTA and economic ties with Russia and the other EAEU countries compatible. A free trade agreement between the EU and the EAEU is one option for doing so, although this is not favored by either the EU or Russia so far, and is technically difficult with regard to Belarus, which is not yet a member of the World Trade Organization (WTO). Alternatively, the in-between states could be encouraged to enter into free trade agreements with both the EU and the EAEU. Indeed, Ukraine and Moldova are already parties to the 2011 CIS free trade agreement, to which all EAEU members are also party. However, Russia withdrew from that regime with regard to Ukraine, and trilateral negotiations among Moscow, Kyiv, and Brussels failed to find agreement on restoring these ties. Moscow should be encouraged to return to these talks and search for a compromise. Another option would be to advance development of compatible regulatory systems and administrative practices between the EU and the EAEU to support the establishment of a more homogeneous shared economic space.

The Commitment to Consult

Future changes in the region could affect the status of the countries in between. As such, these arrangements should create a forum in which all relevant parties would commit to pursue

---

[11] Deep Cuts Commission, *Back from the Brink: Toward Restraint and Dialogue Between Russia and the West*, Institute for Peace Research and Security Policy at the University of Hamburg, June 2016, p. 21.

[12] UN General Assembly, Declaration on Principles of International Law Concerning Friendly Relations and Cooperation Among States in Accordance with the Charter of the United Nations, New York, October 24, 1970.

intensive and inclusive political consultations and dialogue on all issues that may arise from future developments. This should be consistent with the existing OSCE commitment to "[bear] in mind the legitimate security concerns of other States," when exercising the "right freely to choose . . . security arrangements."[13]

Though the proposed arrangement does not grant veto power to countries that may be concerned with the eventual change in the status of nonaligned countries (i.e., Russia), such a consultative commitment should provide a platform to raise concerns and to cooperatively explore possible solutions in good faith. Parties should agree on procedures that would provide assurances to countries that their concerns would be heard and acted upon in a cooperative manner. In the same vein, the agreement should put into place assurances that the mechanism to raise concerns could not be abused for the purpose of obstructing any state's decisions.

The commitment to consult should be extended not only to discussing practical issues that may arise from changing the political-military status of any nonaligned country in between, but also to any eventual future change in their relations with either economic bloc, whether the EU or the EAEU.

Conclusion

Such a combination of East-West understandings and more general undertakings would create more favorable economic and security conditions for the states in between while not foreclosing future membership prospects. It is even possible that some of these in-between states might come to prefer this newly buttressed nonaligned status to membership in an alliance and/or trade bloc, and see it not as a prolonged waystation, but as an enduring status best suited to their needs.

We believe that the proposals above outline a point of departure for de-escalation of the current crisis in European security. Of course, any negotiation on these matters would inevitably enrich the agenda with other related issues. In order to reach an agreement, a highly complex negotiation within different frameworks and engaging different European and Eurasian institutions would be necessary. Such a process would be even more challenging than Russia-West interactions in the 1990s and early 2000s, especially given the deep mistrust that has developed in recent years. As of today, the governments that would have to be party to such a negotiation are very far from acknowledging the need for talks, let alone finding an agreement. Until they are convinced that this option would provide them with a more favorable outcome than the status quo, that is unlikely to change.

---

[13] OSCE, 1994.

CHAPTER THREE

Small Steps: How to Start Improving Security in Europe

Reinhard J. Krumm, Ph.D.
Director, Regional Office for Cooperation and Peace in Europe
Friedrich Ebert Stiftung

The security situation in Europe has returned to an era that many had hoped had passed into history. The situation today, as Eugene Rumer notes, is a "Cold War, Twenty-First-Century Style."[1] Many disagree with the terminology, but regardless of what we call it, the fact remains the West and Russia today are on the verge of a very severe confrontation. Its consequences would be every bit as damaging as the disastrous conflict we feared throughout the Cold War.

How did we get here? The essence of the problem is that there is virtually no trust between Russia and the West—defined here as the EU and the United States. This lack of trust did not develop overnight. Instead, it was to a significant extent a result of the development of the European regional order over the last 25 years. It stems from unfulfilled expectations regarding that order on all sides, as well as almost polar opposite threat perceptions. As a result, almost everyone feels threatened: the West and Russia's neighbors by Russia, and Russia by the United Sates.

This situation is particularly hard on the countries stuck between the West and Russia. Six in-between countries—Armenia, Azerbaijan, Georgia, Belarus, Moldova, and Ukraine—face an unstable status quo. They have all adopted distinct coping strategies. Some of them (Georgia, Moldova, and Ukraine) look toward the West for their future; Belarus seems to have no such aspiration and has become a member of the EAEU and the CSTO. Armenia seeks a middle way; it is a member of the EAEU and CSTO, but is also negotiating an agreement with the EU. Finally, Azerbaijan shows no desire to be aligned with either side.

The fate of these countries has often been a source of contention between Russia and the West. One of the main sources of conflict is the aspiration of Georgia and Ukraine to join NATO, while Russia voices strong concerns about any further enlargement of NATO. On this and other in-between issues, there seems almost no room for compromise, particularly following Russia's annexation of Crimea and invasion of eastern Ukraine and the ensuing Western sanctions against Russia.

The situation is indeed grim, and the trends are not good. But no trend is irreversible. Even if a grand bargain on the European regional order is almost impossible to imagine, we can conceive of immediate concrete steps to improve matters. And such steps might eventually

---

[1]   Eugene Rumer, "Russia and the West in a New Standoff," Carnegie Endowment for International Peace, June 14, 2017.

lead to a way out of the current crisis. Despite all the differences, every country in the region, including Russia, has an interest in achieving better relations with its neighbors.

These steps need to be defined, along with a destination—a "North Star" for orientation—to guide policy and ensure that the steps are aimed at achieving a goal and not wandering all over the map. In other words, we need to ensure a long-term direction for policy decisions made in the short term. We need more than just strategies; we need a process that increases trust among all parties.

Accordingly, this chapter will concentrate more on how to start moving than on the ultimate destination. It will briefly analyze the different expectations of the in-between countries and Russia since the end of the Cold War. It will then introduce the concepts of trust and distrust, providing examples to demonstrate how trust matters in international politics. Finally, the paper will explore how those concepts might suggest ways of moving past the current impasse, with a focus on a process than can create trust rather than on specific solutions to current security problems.

The Evolution of Expectations

Immediately after the end of the Cold War, the security situation in Europe (and the perception of security in Europe) changed dramatically. The newly independent states of Central and Eastern Europe saw a closer relationship with NATO, and eventually membership in the alliance, as the next step in a historical process that had led to the dissolution of the Soviet Union and the end of the Warsaw Pact. Deprived for years of an independent foreign policy, they were eager to make use of their sovereign rights, including their right to join alliances of their choosing.

There was of course also a security concern underpinning that thinking, but this was not linked to any immediate threat. Rather, these states sought a safeguard, a guarantee that history would not repeat itself and that they would not face any future political or military threats to their independence alone. They expected a kind of insurance and general deterrence against future threats, rather than direct NATO efforts to defend against specific threats.

NATO's approach began from different premises. NATO enlargement only began once it became clear that the process would not cause any military conflict or strategic rift on the continent, particularly with Russia. NATO member-states ensured that various stabilizing arrangements, such as the NATO-Russia Founding Act (1997) and the A/CFE (1999), accompanied enlargement. The alliance expected political factors, rather than military considerations, to drive the enlargement process and to ensure the future stability of Europe. They were therefore willing to accept the Baltic states into the alliance, despite the difficulty of militarily defending their territory. Consistent with these premises, NATO simultaneously began a search for a new purpose and mission, focusing on crisis management, out-of-area operations and expeditionary military capabilities. NATO no longer saw defending the territory of its member states as its primary role.

Even in these early years, Russia saw the situation differently. Moscow supported the 1990 Paris Charter for a New Europe specifically because it believed in two crucial clauses in the section entitled "Friendly Relations Among Participating States." The first holds that "[w]ith the ending of the division of Europe, we will strive for a new quality in our security relations, while fully respecting each other's freedom of choice in that respect." The second section touches directly on Russia's security concerns: "[s]ecurity is indivisible and the security of every participating State is inseparably linked to that of all the others."[2] In other words, the principle of the freedom to join alliances was accepted only in the context of a reassurance that changes in alliance memberships do not compromise the security of other states.

Russia made clear its objections to enlargement from the very beginning. Yevgeny Primakov, at the time the head of Russia's foreign intelligence service, and later foreign minister and prime minister, announced Russia's opposition to the eastward enlargement of the Western alliance as early as November 1993. If that were to occur, Primakov said, "the need would arise for a fundamental reappraisal of all defense concepts on our [Russia's] side."[3] During all the years that followed, the oft-repeated Western argument that NATO enlargement was not directed against Russia did little to assuage Moscow's concerns.

Those post-communist countries that did not join NATO and the EU see the European regional order in yet another way. Among those "in-betweens," there are a variety of different levels of ambition for the relationship with NATO and the EU. There is, however, one common denominator: Each of them sees its relations with NATO, whatever its aim (membership, cooperation, political affiliation, partnership, or simply access to NATO deliberations) as a policy instrument for influencing its own citizens. In other words, the expectations of the in-between countries are linked to their domestic politics. For example, decision makers in Tbilisi are very much in tune with Georgian citizens in their hopes to join the EU, whereas decisionmakers in Minsk are in agreement with the Belarusian population in not wanting to join the EU.[4]

There are important differences in how these states see their relationship with the West. Some of the in-between states clearly want military protection. Ukraine and Georgia hope that NATO would come to their defense against a Russian military threat to their independence or territorial integrity. They see NATO as a security policy instrument and a tool for defending themselves against Russia. If the conflicts (Crimea, Donbas, Abkhazia, and South Ossetia) that are currently plaguing these states were to end, their security policy choices might change over time, depending on Russian behavior.

Finally, some in-between states, such as Armenia, Azerbaijan, and Belarus, often see Western institutions as sources of political leverage with Russia or with each other. In this context, the relationship with those institutions is treated as an instrument of foreign policy. Belarus seeks to position itself as "bridge" between East and West. Similarly, Armenia and Azerbaijan in their dealings with the Nagorno-Karabakh conflict often seek to involve Western institutions in order to gain leverage vis-à-vis each other or Russia.

All of this implies that not all of these states wish to join NATO and the EU. Therefore, there is no one-size-fits-all solution or arrangement which can satisfy all of them. But beyond the question of membership, the fundamental problem remains that if the in-between states do not get what they want—NATO or EU membership, or whatever alternative solution they desire—they will continue to feel insecure and, in their difficult interaction with Russia and the West, they will continue to create security problems in Europe.

---

[2]   OSCE, 1990.

[3]   Steven Erlanger, "Russia Warns NATO On Expanding East," *New York Times*, November 26, 1993.

[4]   See International Republican Institute, *Survey of Public Opinion in Georgia*, February 22–March 8, 2017, and Elena A. Korosteleva, "Belarus Between the European Union and the Eurasian Economic Union," ODB Brussels, 2016.

Trust and Distrust

These distinct expectations and desires help explain the mistrust among Russia and some of the in-between countries as well as between Russia and the West. There is a lack of transparency of intentions—every side suspects hidden hostile motives behind every action. This is compounded by uncertainty about the future. Russia worries about a possible drive for further NATO enlargement, and the in-between states, the EU, and the United States have at least as many questions about Russia concerning its quest for "privileged interests" in its neighboring countries. All sides deny any malicious intentions.

Peter Ustinov's Cold War satire *Romanoff and Juliet* demonstrates how damaging (and absurd) this situation can be. An official from a Central European country is trying to discover the intentions of the United States and the Soviet Union toward his "in-between" country. Both states are officially saying one thing, but intending something else to deceive the other side. At the end, the official tells the American ambassador: "Incidentally, you know—they know you know they know you know." To which the American ambassador, genuinely alarmed, asks: "What? Are you sure?"[5]

According to the Nash equilibrium, a foundational concept in game theory, two actors who each know each other's strategy have little incentive to change their own strategy—simply because there is no guarantee that if one changes one's own strategy to find compromise, the other actor will change strategy reciprocally. To make progress, trust and a way to verify the promised changes are necessary. Either one views trust as a prerequisite for improving relations and working on substantial agreements, or one views the act of working on substantial shared results via agreed frameworks as a means of building trust in the first place. We favor the second option. That implies mechanisms are needed to begin creating substantial on-the-ground results in the absence of trust. There are different ways to create these mechanisms, such as "rais[ing] the costs of untrustworthy conduct" through sanctions or deterrence or offering one-sided concessions to gain trust.[6] The risk of such an initiative is much higher and means "raising the vulnerability of the benevolent partner."[7] This paper endorses a positive strategy—seeking cooperation on less important issues, thus creating islands of cooperation that might ultimately expand.

In the case of the "in-between" countries, the OSCE could take on this role, since all the relevant parties are members of the organization. Moreover, the OSCE's predecessor, the CSCE, played a major role in building trust during the Cold War, starting with the Helsinki Final Act in 1975, as well as with the above-mentioned Paris Charter of 1990. The chairmanships of the OSCE in 2016 (Germany) and 2017 (Austria) have given a much-needed impetus to an organization which has long sought a role in the post-Cold War era. Now is a good moment to try to use the OSCE as a platform for rebuilding the trust that is so urgently required, while recognizing that the organization will not ever be able to realize the CSCE's lofty aspirations of being the primary forum for discussions regarding European security.

Public opinion surveys show that trust is mostly absent in relations between the "in-betweens" and Russia. Trust with Russia is particularly lacking for the three states that have

---

5   *Romanoff and Juliet*, dir. Peter Ustinov, Universal Studios, 1961.

6   Piotr Sztompka, "Two Theoretical Approaches to Trust: Their Implications for the Resolution of Intergroup Conflict," in Ilai Alon and Daniel Bar-Tal, eds., *The Role of Trust in Conflict Resolution*, Cham, Switzerland: Springer, 2016, pp. 15–21.

7   Sztompka, 2016.

signed AAs with the EU: Georgia, Moldova and Ukraine. In all three countries, relations with Russia are seen as poor to various degrees (in Georgia, 77 percent; in Ukraine, 58 percent; and in Moldova, 41 percent).[8] Still, it is noteworthy that even in Georgia an overwhelming majority (83 percent) are supportive or somewhat supportive of further dialogue with Russia.[9] Under these circumstances, the best thing one can imagine is to loosen the knot of distrust between the relevant actors by taking small steps. But how?

Concrete Steps: Islands of Cooperation and Structured Dialogue

The regional order is at a crossroads. A strategy that proposed immediate, concrete solutions might seem preferable to the elaboration of a process that will only lead to stability over time. But since outcomes depend so much on process, the emphasis here will be on concrete steps that move in the right direction. Three fundamental paths present themselves: the current direction, which is counterproductive and, at least for some countries, unsustainable; an extreme one that involves increased confrontation and increased risk of conflict; and an evolutionary path, which is the one laid out in the following paragraphs.

It makes little sense to continue on the current path. As Michael E. O'Hanlon puts it, "We have arguably created the worst of all worlds." He argues that NATO membership seems to have become the most important goal for some countries, even though that very membership might put their security at risk: "We have inadvertently built a type of NATO membership doomsday machine that raises the likelihood of conflict in Europe."[10] The West and Russia can perhaps afford to continue along the current path. But for many of the in-between countries, particularly Georgia, Moldova and Ukraine, the status quo is less sustainable. The three countries are at risk of ever greater political and economic instability.

The second path would mean abandoning all efforts to create a shared regional order that all parties, including Russia, could accept. In that case, foreign policymakers would have to deal with an obstructionist Russia that has no hope of any cooperation with the EU or the United States. This strategy would seek to exhaust Russia so that it was less capable of aggression. But "success" in this case could lead to an imploding nuclear superpower and thus perhaps create even greater security threats than the status quo.

The third path would be based upon the understanding that relations among states are never easy and need constant tending. The relevant parties would have to agree on a "North Star" for orientation, an ultimate goal of a stable and secure regional order that all parties, including Russia, could accept. To begin the process, one should agree that trust-building measures could start immediately and need not require demonstrations of "good behavior" upfront. For now, a grand bargain is very unlikely, so it makes sense to take small, well-defined

---

[8]   The Public Opinion Surveys of residents were conducted on behalf of the International Republican Institute. See International Republican Institute, *Public Opinion Survey Residents Surveys of Georgia*, March–April 2016a; International Republican Institute, *Public Opinion Survey Residents of Ukraine*, May–June 2016b; and International Republican Institute, *Public Opinion Survey Residents Surveys of Moldova*, September 2016c.

[9]   International Republican Institute, 2016a, 2016b, 2016c.

[10]   Michael E. O'Hanlon, "Beyond NATO: A New Security Architecture for Eastern Europe," Brookings Institution, July 28, 2017.

steps.[11] Small steps make sense when one understands that their purpose is not to restore trust and cooperation in general but simply to begin the process. Moreover, the costs of failure are low—the situation will not get worse for trying.

There are several ways of pursuing a policy of small steps. One is to find an island of cooperation in a limited and small-scale area. This cooperation should involve issues of mutual interest, rather than potential or real conflicts. There are good examples of such efforts within the region, which are useful for illustration. These are mostly economically motivated initiatives from countries that have had more reason to seek cooperation. For example, Georgia established the institution of a special envoy for relations with Russia. They initiated bilateral talks and realized some increase in trade, especially of wine, followed by an improvement in the cooperation between the transport authorities of the two countries.[12] Clearly, both countries were and are interested in these developments. This approach of bilateral talks with Russia could be very useful for other countries.

Another example is the breakaway Moldovan region of Transnistria, which decided in 2016 to comply with the DCFTA that is part of the AA between Moldova and the EU.[13] After a long period of opposition to the DCFTA, mainly economic interests motivated the policy shift. The economic situation in Moldova had been worsening and there was little prospect that Russia, struggling under Western sanctions, would compensate Transnistria if it did not comply with the DCFTA.

Another category of small steps involves merely opening up dialogue on sensitive issues where interests clash. Such a dialogue should be structured and inclusive, with neutral observers monitoring progress. Such an effort is underway in the framework of the OSCE. Under the auspices of the Declaration on the 20th Anniversary of the OSCE Framework for Arms Control, adopted in Hamburg in 2016, the OSCE participating states initiated a structured dialogue to discuss topics such as diverging threat perceptions, different military doctrines and trends in military capabilities.[14] The short-term goal is to bring all parties back to the negotiating table; the long-term goal is resumption of conventional arms control negotiations in Europe.

The EU and the EAEU could also initiate a separate structured dialogue. The aim would be to find common interests and begin working on concrete projects. A report on Russian foreign policy, initiated by a think tank close to former Russian finance minister Alexei Kudrin, supports the initiation of such cooperation and suggests depoliticizing the dialogue between

---

[11] U.S. President John F. Kennedy formulated a similar approach at the height of the Cold War in 1963. In a speech titled "Strategy of Peace," the president expressly noted that he wasn't seeking a "grand or magic formula" but "a series of concrete actions and effective agreements which are in the interests of all concerned." John F. Kennedy, "Commencement Address at American University in Washington," The American Presidency Project, June 10, 1963.

[12] Paata Gaprindashvili, "How to Improve Russia-Georgia Talks?" in *Georgia and Russia: In Search of Ways for Normalization*, Tbilisi: Georgian Foundation for Strategic and International Studies, 2017, pp. 5–11.

[13] Guillaume Van der Loo, "The EU's Association Agreements and DCFTAs with Ukraine, Moldova and Georgia: A Comparative Study," Center for European Policy Studies, Brussels, June 24, 2017.

[14] OSCE, "From Lisbon to Hamburg: Declaration on the Twentieth Anniversary of the OSCE Framework for Arms Control," Organization for Security and Co-operation in Europe Ministerial Council, Hamburg, December 9, 2016.

the EU and EAEU.[15] (For more on possible cooperation, see the paper by Ademmer and Lissovolik in this volume.)

Such a structured dialogue would benefit all relevant parties. The in-between states want to get out of the current unsustainable situation and need to think about a stable environment for developing their economies and particularly trade. The EU is interested in stabilizing its neighborhood, and Russia desperately needs a way out of the costly and burdensome conflict in the Donbas region. If the sides could make progress on these issues, that success would build trust to enable joint medium-term policy initiatives (see some ideas in the chapter by Dobbins and Zagorski in this volume). For all the parties, such talks also have the advantage of continuous communication regarding intentions and perceptions of other parties.

The concept of islands of cooperation will only succeed if such islands serve as a genuine confidence-building process, even if a long-term one. The approach will not work if presented (by Moscow or anyone else) as yet another means of confronting the West's ambitions to expand its institutions to the east. In other words, cooperating with Moscow cannot come at the cost of forever foreclosing the Western aspirations of the in-between states, even if such aspirations remain out of reach for now. The discussion on security arrangements for in-betweens should focus more on their actual security, and less on their institutional affiliation. The question with which they need to grapple is whether, for them, NATO or EU membership is the only possible instrument to preserve their sovereignty or territorial integrity or whether they would be ready to use other policy instruments to achieve the same goal.

More concretely, confidence and security-building measures (CSBMs) represent an important opportunity to improve the circumstances of the in-between states and regional security generally: establishing bilateral CSBMs between Russia and individual in-betweens, as envisaged in Chapter X of the 2011 Vienna Document.[16] This chapter envisions creating measures beyond those contained in that document, but remaining in line with their spirit. Given the current situation in Donbas and the status of Crimea, this would not work for Russia and Ukraine right now. However, the withdrawal component of the Minsk Agreements was based on a CSCE/OSCE document, the 1993 Stabilizing Measures for Localized Crisis Situations and with a certain amount of political will the Minsk Agreements could evolve into full-fledged CSBMs.[17] Given the difficult circumstances faced by the residents of the Donbas, economic confidence-building measures for the benefit of the local population should accompany or follow military CSBMs.

A regional order that all parties could accept seems a distant prospect. But that was also the case in the 1960s, after the construction of the Berlin Wall. And it was true too during the CSCE process in the 1970s, which faced numerous obstacles from the start. In those moments, trust was lacking but the sides did not consider trust to be a precondition for starting and continuing negotiating processes. Even the Soviet invasion of Afghanistan (1979) or the shooting down of a civilian Korean Airlines jet (1983) did not stop the ongoing talks between East and West.

---

[15] Ivan Timofeev, *Theses on Russia's Foreign Policy and Global Positioning (2017–2024)*, Moscow: Center for Strategic Research, June 2017.

[16] OSCE, Vienna Document 2011: On Confidence- And Security-Building Measures, Vienna, November 30, 2011.

[17] OSCE, Stabilizing Measures for Localized Crisis Situations, Vienna, November 25, 1993.

As Adam Gopnik writes, "[g]etting out to make good things happen beats sitting down and thinking big things up."[18] We do not know how to make a grand bargain. But let us not sit down. We need to initiate a process of new thinking on regional integration in Europe and Eurasia to reverse the current, dangerous trajectory and to see where that process takes us. Taking well-defined small steps that seek to form islands of cooperation and beginning structured dialogues are good ways to start.

---

[18] Adam Gopnik, "Are Liberals on the Wrong Side of History?" *The New Yorker,* March 20, 2017.

CHAPTER FOUR

Thoughts on Inclusive Economic Integration

Esther Ademmer, Ph.D.
Post-Doctoral Researcher
Kiel Institute for the World Economy

Yaroslav Lissovolik, Ph.D.
Chief Economist, Member of the Management Board
Eurasian Development Bank

Improved trade relations with neighbors are vitally important for the economies of states located in between the two customs unions of the EU and the EAEU. Both economic theory and analyses of trade relationships between the EAEU, the EU and the countries between these customs unions suggest that an improvement in mutual trade relationships would provide for dynamism and growth prospects for all parties.[1] However, current tensions among states in the region prevent the benefits of improved trade relations from being realized. On the contrary, political, economic, and outright military conflict erupted when countries such as Georgia, Moldova, and Ukraine were confronted with mutually exclusive economic integration agreements by the EU and the EAEU of Russia, Belarus, Kazakhstan, Armenia, and Kyrgyzstan.

Both EU and EAEU members and countries located between the two blocs have regularly felt that "red lines" are being crossed and seemingly technical matters, such as food safety requirements, have morphed into explosive political disputes. Although the impact of the sanctions imposed since 2014 by Russia and the West on trade flows is still hotly debated,[2] the deterioration of the broader relationship has rendered the vision of a free trade area from Lisbon to Vladivostok, which many actors on both sides had once hoped to establish, a pipe dream.[3] Cooperative attempts to resolve economic elements of the broader post-2014 crisis, as

---

[1] G.R. Felbermayr, R. Aichele, and J. Gröschl, *Freihandel von Lissabon Nach Wladiwostok: Wem Nutzt, Wem Schadet Ein Eurasisches Freihandelsabkommen?* Munich: Ifo Institut, 2016.

[2] Matthieu Crozet and Julian Hinz, *Collateral Damage: The Impact of The Russia Sanctions on Sanctioning Countries' Exports*, CEPII Working Paper, Vol. 59, 2016; Christian Dreger, Konstantin A. Kholodilin, Dirk Ulbricht, and Jarko Fidrmuc, "Between the Hammer and the Anvil: The Impact of Economic Sanctions and Oil Prices on Russia's Ruble," *Journal of Comparative Economics*, Vol. 44, No. 2, 2016, pp. 295–308; Francesco Giumelli, "The Redistributive Impact of Restrictive Measures on EU Members: Winners and Losers from Imposing Sanctions on Russia," *Journal of Common Market Studies*, Vol. 55, No. 5, 2017, pp. 1062–1080; K. A. Kholodilin and A. Netsunajev, "Crimea And Punishment: The Impact of Sanctions on Russian and European Economies," DIW Discussion Paper, Vol. 1569, 2016.

[3] Rilka Dragneva and Kataryna Wolczuk, "The EU-Ukraine Association Agreement and the Challenges of Inter-Regionalism," *Review of Central and East European Law*, Vol. 39, 2014, pp. 213–244; Auswärtiges Amt, "Rede von Sta-

in the case of trilateral talks between Russia, the EU, and Ukraine on the latter's DCFTA, have failed. As a result, regional economic integration is now largely considered a zero-sum game.

Most appraisals of recent developments in the region approach these issues with normative judgements of the role of the EU or Russia in this crisis. More analytical perspectives assess the compatibility of the two integration endeavors and point to the fact that countries "squeezed" between both customs unions are also agents in their own right.[4] This paper approaches the problem from such an analytical stance. It is the result of a longer process of exchanges and debates between the authors of this paper and the wider working group. While we differ in our respective assessments of the origins of the current crisis, we share the view that the current situation needs to be ameliorated. This paper has thus been explicitly designed to be forward-looking and geared at proposing a process towards finding solutions. Though we are aware that the economic area is most likely not the source of the problem, we suggest that it may still be a sphere where more constructive dynamics are possible. We recommend starting and/or continuing building bilateral economic cooperation agreements between differently integrated economies in the region to interlock states in the region economically and create synergies where possible. We suggest that such steps might help grow partnerships as well as domestic institutions that can eventually handle complex trade relationships and facilitate the emergence of rule-based economic integration mechanisms. Additionally, we propose that the commissions of the EU and the EAEU simultaneously begin a dialogue to pave the way for more inclusive regional economic integration. The paper begins by outlining some of the specific economic challenges that are associated with the competition between the regional integration projects of the EU and the EAEU, and then offers recommendations to contribute to the creation of a more inclusive economic order in the region.

The Challenge of Inclusive Economic Integration

From a purely economic point of view, inclusive economic integration in the region appears feasible at first sight. The establishment of a free trade area between the EU and EAEU would address the economic incompatibilities and the existing mutually exclusive character of their offerings to prospective partners. A recent study of such a scenario found that a comprehensive free trade agreement reducing tariff and nontariff barriers (NTBs) between the EU and the EAEU would be highly economically beneficial for all parties involved.[5] Furthermore, economic integration within the EAEU has been based on the EU experience and WTO rules.[6] Due to its greater legality and more rigorous institutionalized setting, the EAEU and its precursor, the Eurasian Customs Union, were initially considered to be a leap forward in structur-

---

atssekretär Markus Ederer beim Jahresempfang des Ost-Ausschusses der Deutschen Wirtschaft: 'Eurasien-Brennpunkt der Interessen oder Raum der Kooperation?'" webpage, 2017.

[4]   C. Nitoiu, "European and Eurasian Integration: Competition and Cooperation in the Post-Soviet Space," *Journal of European Integration*, Vol. 39, No. 4, 2017, pp. 469–475.

[5]   Felbermayr et al., 2016.

[6]   Richard Connolly, "Russia, the Eurasian Customs Union and the WTO," in Rilka Dragneva and Kataryna Wolczuk, eds., *Eurasian Economic Integration: Law, Policy and Politics*, Cheltenham: Edward Elgar, 2013, pp. 61–78.

ing rules-based cooperation in the post-Soviet space.[7] However, the current political situation makes it nearly impossible to achieve such a "Lisbon to Vladivostok" scenario between the EAEU and the EU in the medium term.

While the DCFTA with the EU is compatible with standard free trade agreements (FTAs), such as the one established in the framework of the CIS, joining the EAEU and signing a DCFTA with the EU are mutually exclusive steps.[8] Whereas membership in a customs union like the EAEU deprives member states of their sovereign prerogative to set external tariffs and NTBs, a DCFTA requires the signatory to exercise this prerogative to lower tariffs and NTBs. The result of this clash was best illustrated in the case of Armenia: Yerevan's decision to join the Eurasian Customs Union in September 2013 prevented the Armenian authorities from adjusting their tariffs and NTBs as foreseen in the EU-Armenia DCFTA, which had been finalized in July 2013. As a result, the agreement was scrapped.

Additional economic concerns were associated with the impact of the DCFTA for signatories' established trade partners. The DCFTA aims at boosting trade relations between the EU and EaP countries through the latter's agreement to adopt a large part of EU's *acquis communautaire*, its body of laws and regulations, which covers a wide array of issues such as competition policy, food safety, and technical standards. This regulatory alignment was designed to stimulate the economies of these countries in the long run, due not only to the promotion of trade with the EU, but also by having an enabling effect on trade with other countries which accept EU-certified products.[9] However, the EU standards were introduced in place of existing standards agreed in the context of the CIS. According to the provisions of the DCFTA, horizontal standards and procedures—along with tariffs—contained in the agreement must be adopted at the national level and alternative regulatory standards need to be phased out. Russia has argued that DCFTA signatories' adoption of EU standards would hinder its trade with these states. While Moscow has not identified specific goods that would be affected, it is not implausible that as DCFTA signatories align their standards toward the EU and away from Russia, trade with the former will be facilitated while trade with the latter will be complicated. In principle, however, conflicting standards can be renegotiated or mutually accommodated, but thus far attempts to do so have failed.[10]

As a trade partner of many DCFTA countries, Russia additionally feared that its markets would be flooded with EU products that are shipped via those countries. Such issues are regulated by WTO rules of origin, however.[11] With the exception of Belarus, all EAEU and

[7]   Rilka Dragneva, "The Legal and Institutional Dimensions of The Eurasian Customs Union," in Rilka Dragneva and Kataryna Wolczuk, eds., *Eurasian Economic Integration: Law, Policy and Politics*, Cheltenham: Edward Elgar, 2013, pp. 34–60.

[8]   László Bruszt and Julia Langbein, "Varieties of Dis-Embedded Liberalism: EU Integration Strategies in the Eastern Peripheries of Europe," *Journal of European Public Policy*, Vol. 24, No. 2, 2017, pp. 297–315.

[9]   Amat Adarov and Peter Havlik, "Benefits and Costs of DCFTA: Evaluation of the Impact on Georgia, Moldova, and Ukraine," Joint Working Paper of WIIW and Bertelsmann Stiftung, Vienna Institute for International Economic Studies, 2016.

[10]   Evgeny Vinokurov, Peter Balas, Michael Emerson, Peter Havlik, Vladimir Pereboyev, Elena Rovenskaya, Anastasia Stepanova, Jurij Kofner, and Pavel Kabat, "Non-Tariff Barriers and Technical Regulations," IIASA Workshop Report, Laxenburg: International Institute for Applied Systems Analysis, 2016.

[11]   See Michael Emerson, "Russia's Economic Interests and the EU's DCFTA with Ukraine," EurActiv.com, June 2014.

EU members, as well as Ukraine, Georgia, Armenia, and Moldova, are WTO members. Such problems should thus not arise if existing WTO rules were correctly applied.

While technical solutions may thus generally be found in the area of economics and a corpus of WTO rules formally governs trade relationships, the poor implementation of such principles, rules, and mechanisms challenges inclusive economic integration in the region. Apart from political considerations, this problem is also linked to the capacity of states to put complex trade agreements and rules into practice.[12]

Ideas on How to Create Order

The goal of this project is to suggest ways to forge a stable regional order for the countries located between Russia and the West. Order in this sense is defined as a "stable, structured pattern of relationships among states" which should augment, not replace existing institutions.[13] The idea is to suggest a framework to address economic challenges and exploit economic potential, create rules by which external actors should abide, anchor respect for international agreements and principles, and eventually generate trust and cooperation between the EU, Russia, and their common neighbors. We suggest negotiation of bilateral agreements to interlock economies, flanked by mechanisms to initiate inclusive dialogue between the commissions of the EU and the EAEU and other countries in the region.

Bilaterally Interlocking Economies, Building Institutions

Both the EU and the EAEU rules allow for the blocs to sign agreements with other states and customs unions. The Treaty on the Eurasian Economic Union provides for the possibility of creating free trade zones between the EAEU and third parties, and does not preclude member-states of the union from signing other international agreements, as long as they are in line with the purposes and principles of the treaty.[14] Further, any country that is not part of a customs union like the EU or EAEU may enter into as many classic FTAs as it wants to. This is true for the countries in the region that have signed a DCFTA with the EU: Ukraine, Georgia and Moldova. Likewise, the EU DCFTAs do not preclude signatories from concluding other trade agreements, except if they conflict with the DCFTA. The DCFTA commits parties to consult before entering into other trade agreements.[15]

Negotiating bilateral economic agreements can be used as a way to build trust between states. The coexistence of various bilateral agreements would ideally interlock economies in a way that makes individual countries consider relationships with other trade blocs when enacting changes in their existing trade arrangements. If designed accordingly, they may also help to build more sustainable institutional structures in Eurasia to boost growth and the delivery

---

[12] Adarov and Havlik, 2016; Connolly, 2013; Dragneva and Wolczuk, 2014; J. Langbein, *Transnationalization and Regulatory Change in the EU's Eastern Neighbourhood*, London: Routledge, 2015.

[13] Michael J. Mazarr, Miranda Priebe, Andrew Radin, and Astrid Stuth Cevallos, *Understanding the Current International Order*, Santa Monica, Calif.: RAND Corporation, RR-1598-OSD, 2016.

[14] Eurasian Economic Union, Treaty on the Eurasian Economic Union, Astana, May 29, 2014.

[15] EU, Association Agreement Between the European Union and The European Atomic Energy Community and Their Member States, of the One Part, and the Republic of Moldova, of the Other Part, Brussels, June 27, 2014.

of public goods and services; and at the same time facilitate cooperation among regional integration institutions.

Bilateral agreements based on such a variable geometry approach are beginning to emerge already. For example, recent developments in Armenia illustrate how economic relations can develop between EAEU members and the EU. As noted above, Armenia had finalized the text of a DCFTA with the EU in the summer of 2013, but in September of that year, Yerevan announced its intention to join the Eurasian Customs Union and the EU-Armenia DCFTA was scrapped as a result. Armenia eventually joined the Eurasian Customs Union, and in January 2015 became a member of its successor, the EAEU. Despite this, Armenia and the EU initialed a new framework agreement on comprehensive partnership on March 21, 2017. The document differs significantly from the DCFTA agreement, and must remain in line with Armenia's EAEU obligations. Nevertheless, the agreement does address economic and investment cooperation. The agreement excludes trade in goods in light of Armenia's membership in the EAEU, but covers a variety of other areas, such as energy, transport, the environment, public procurement, and intellectual property rights.[16] The agreement complements existing EAEU agreements, and links the EU-Armenian economies in a variety of sectors. It also puts a strong emphasis on the rule of law and on improving the regulatory environment for businesses, which may help to create the capacity and conditions for rules-based economic cooperation.

The hope of interlocking economies in various areas across blocs would be that those states subsequently take the interest of their partners into account when changing existing trade relationships. Such complex forms of interdependence, however, do not necessarily lead to more cooperation.[17] In the case of Armenia, for instance, there is no clear-cut mechanism to deal with potentially conflicting commitments towards the EU and the EAEU: A general carve-out clause that would have allowed Armenia to opt out of commitments in case they may conflict with its EAEU commitments in the future was rejected by the EU.[18] In the event that EAEU or EU integration deepens in a way that is incompatible with Armenia's commitments to the other bloc, renewed disagreement is likely if there are no mechanisms to prevent such conflicts in the first place. As such, inclusive institutions that mediate potential conflicts arising from changes in economic integration patterns are needed.

Inclusive Institutions and Inter-Regional Economic Relations

The key institution to mediate trade-related conflicts is the WTO. It has a clear set of rules for resolving trade disputes and foresees negotiations and potential compensation mechanisms for those states that are negatively affected by deeper regional trade integration of fellow WTO members. Prior consultations about the expansion of customs unions with affected parties form part of a standard practice of the WTO. According to WTO norms, countries affected by a given WTO member's formation of a customs union (involving increases in bound duty

---

[16] EU External Action Service, "Joint Press Release by the European Union and Republic of Armenia on the Initialing of the EU-Armenia Comprehensive and Enhanced Partnership Agreement," Brussels, March 21, 2017; "Mogherini's Spokesperson Calls New EU-Armenia Agreement 'Ambitious," Mediamax.am, 2017.

[17] R. O. Keohane and J. S. Nye, "Power and Interdependence Revisited," *International Organization,* Vol. 41, No. 4, 1987, pp. 725–753.

[18] H. Kostanyan and R. Giragosian, "EU-Armenian Relations: Seizing the Second Chance," *CEPS Commentary*, October 2016.

rates) must first negotiate compensation with that country before existing concessions can be withdrawn.

For instance, compensation was provided for the EU enlargements in 2004 and 2007. Apart from the United States, WTO members that sought compensation from the EU as a result of the 2004 enlargement included Argentina, Australia, Brazil, Canada, Costa Rica, Colombia, Ecuador, Guatemala, India, Japan, Malaysia, New Zealand, Pakistan, Panama, the Philippines, South Korea, Taiwan, Thailand, and Uruguay.[19] In March 2006, the United States and the EU signed a bilateral agreement providing for compensation resulting from the enlargement.[20] Under the agreement, the EU introduced new tariff-rate quotas for U.S. exports of boneless ham, poultry, and corn gluten meal; expanded global tariff-rate quotas, including for food preparations, fructose, pork, rice, barley, wheat, maize, and fruit juices; and reduced tariffs on protein concentrates, fish, aluminum, tube and molybdenum wire.

The WTO recently served as a framework by which to address concerns of the EU, the United States, Japan, and other WTO members linked to Armenia's accession to the EAEU. Additionally, Russia appealed to the WTO regarding its concerns about Ukraine's DCFTA.[21] Likewise, the EU, Russia and Ukraine have sought to settle several trade disputes with one another since 2013 using WTO mechanisms. As such, the WTO can serve as a tool to resolve the concerns of states negatively affected by the accession of a WTO member to the EAEU or the DCFTA.

Nonetheless, the WTO mechanisms may not be able to address all economic conflicts in the region. First, unlike the EU, the EAEU is not itself a member of the WTO, nor is its member-state Belarus. Azerbaijan and Serbia, two other countries in the region, are also not members of the WTO. Serbia is an EU accession candidate and is negotiating an FTA with the EAEU. Encouraging the WTO accession of these countries may help to make sure that there is an institutional backbone to deal with disputes in the long run. Joining the WTO would also require substantial reforms of these countries' domestic institutional and economic systems, which may help strengthen enforcement and compliance with established rules. However, WTO accession processes can be lengthy and are unlikely to provide for a straightforward short- or medium-term solution.

In the past, the EU and Russia also managed concerns about the regional economic integration of third countries. Under the aegis of the EU-Russia Partnership and Cooperation Agreement, the economic implications of the EU's 2004 enlargement were discussed and eventually the sides signed an agreement whereby the EU made compensatory tariff adjustments.[22] Today, the political climate makes it highly unlikely that such a bilateral negotiation format will be revived in the short term. In addition, the multilateral economic relations at stake in Eurasia are more complex today, as the EAEU is formally in charge of trade policy issues for its member states, while Georgia, Moldova, and Ukraine are not members of either the EU or the EAEU. All parties need to be at the table when their respective economic relations are

---

[19] International Center for Trade and Sustainable Development, "WTO Challenges Emerge over EU Expansion," *Bridges*, Vol. 8, No. 33, 2004.

[20] U.S. Trade Representative, "EU Enlargement," USTR.gov, undated.

[21] WTO, "Council for Trade in Goods," November 17, 2014.

[22] EU, "EU Council Press Release: Joint Statement on EU Enlargement and EU-Russia Relations," Luxembourg: April 2004. See also Jackie Gower, "EU-Russian Relations and the Eastern Enlargement: Integration or Isolation?" *Perspectives on European Politics and Society*, Vol. 1, Issue 1, 2000.

concerned. Still, both analysts and policymakers should be aware of the positive precedent set in 2004: Such talks are not only possible to hold, but it is also possible to find agreement.

We recommend using the coexistence of regional integration efforts in Eurasia as the basis for starting a more inclusive economic dialogue between the EU and the EAEU, as an attempt to circumvent current zero-sum dynamics. This dialogue could be institutionalized between the commissions of both the EU and the EAEU and might eventually lead to negotiations about inter-regional economic cooperation—whatever form it may take. This may also provide for a more open institutional backbone to generate cooperative and more inclusive momentum in the region.

The suggestion of starting such a dialogue is certainly not new and neither are the concerns about it.[23] The EU has so far been highly reluctant to establish formal relations with EAEU bodies, despite the fact that it has usually been a major promoter of other regional integration projects around the globe.[24] Its reluctance is the result of several underlying issues. First, many in the EU have argued that dialogue about more technical issues is unlikely to solve the underlying political problems and rather legitimizes Russia's foreign policy actions (to which the EU strongly objects).[25] Second, any attempts of the EU and EAEU to negotiate an FTA face legal constraints due to the fact that Belarus is not a member of the WTO.[26] And third, despite the fact that the EAEU has been modelled on the EU's institutional structure, there are substantial differences in their functioning and some thus argue that they are not appropriate partners.[27]

We posit that despite these reservations, it is worthwhile to open a channel of communication between both commissions. As a first step, this could be designed as a simple diplomatic effort between the two organizations formally representing all members of the respective customs unions. Fears of Russia's denying its EAEU partners a voice in such talks should be allayed by the union's procedures; despite the fact that Russia is by far the largest economy in the organization, it does not enjoy privileged voting rights.[28] In this case, mandates for talks with the EU would need to be granted to the EAEU Commission by all the respective member states. If an institution representing all EAEU member states on one side, and another representing EU states on the other entered into a dialogue, there is a chance that their interaction could strengthen and legitimize more-depoliticized bodies and boost the consolidation of internal procedures and commitments. With more technocratic and rules-based mechanisms in the fore, there is a better chance that disputes could be resolved pragmatically.

The lowest common denominator for such an effort would most likely be basic information exchange on economic issues (something that is already possible today), following the

---

[23] Rilka Dragneva-Lewers and Kataryna Wolczuk, "Trade and Geopolitics: Should the EU Engage with the Eurasian Economic Union?" *EPC Policy Brief*, April 2, 2015; Nitoiu, 2017.

[24] F. Söderbaum, P. Stålgren, and Van L. Langenhove, "The EU as a Global Actor and the Dynamics of Interregionalism: A Comparative Analysis," *Journal of European Integration*, Vol. 27, No. 3, 2005, pp. 365–380.

[25] Dragneva and Wolczuk, 2015.

[26] Won-Mog Choi, "Legal Problems of Making Regional Trade Agreements with Non-WTO-Member States," *Journal of International Economic Law*, Vol. 8, No. 4, 2005, pp. 825–860.

[27] Rilka Dragneva and Kataryna Wolczuk, *The Eurasian Economic Union: Deals, Rules and the Exercise of Power*, London: Chatham House, 2017; Vinokurov et al., 2016.

[28] Dragneva, 2013; A. Libman, "Russian Power Politics and the Eurasian Economic Union: The Real and the Imagined," *Rising Powers Quarterly*, Vol. 2, No. 1, 2017, pp. 81–103.

EU's formal recognition of the EAEU, a step Brussels has thus far not been prepared to take. Recognition could create political momentum to negotiate, agree, and adhere to guiding principles for economic cooperation and transparency. The dialogue could initially provide a platform for returning to the negotiation table and debating issues that jointly affect member states of either customs union, such as in the case of potential future incompatibilities arising from Armenia's recent agreement with the EU.

If fruitful, such a dialogue may eventually help to expose islands of economic cooperation. Potential areas for cooperation are far reaching, and do not necessarily need to cover trade.[29] Cooperation could also be enhanced between development institutions such as the European Bank for Reconstruction and Development (EBRD) and the Eurasian Development Bank (EDB) to support projects that may help to initiate specific forms of cooperation and further common economic goals, such as infrastructure development. This cooperation could take the form of formal cooperation via memoranda and agreements to include project co-financing in the in-between countries.[30] There is scope to explore such projects in Armenia and Belarus (who are already members in both institutions) or in Moldova, for example, if Moldova were to pursue membership in the EDB. Eventually, EU-EAEU dialogue could also encompass capacity-building to foster rule-based regional economic integration.

If this approach is successful, it could serve as an organizational forum that may be extended to allow for trilateral consultations with additional partners in the region. Parties requesting trilateral consultations because they suspect their economic interests to be affected by bilateral trade agreements would need to document concrete negative repercussions they anticipate might result from trade or deepening economic relations with the respective third party. A mechanism of this nature could also be used to facilitate information sharing and transparency, without violating the right of any state or customs union to deepen economic ties with third parties. Conditions for such consultations would be negotiated between the commissions (based on a respective mandate by all member states) and the third country *ex ante*.

We certainly acknowledge that the success of our proposals is far from certain. However, we can say with a high degree of certainty that the status quo is not a viable, sustainable alternative. Initiating the dialogue we recommend would provide a chance to build some trust and thereby inject constructive dynamics into a region that sorely needs it.

---

[29] Vinokurov et al., 2016.

[30] All EU and EAEU members and in-between countries belong to the EBRD; membership in the EDB is open to all countries and does not depend on membership in the EAEU.

CHAPTER FIVE

Approaches to Resolving the Conflict over the States In Between

Ambassador Oleksandr Chalyi
President
Grant Thornton Ukraine

Defining "In-Between"

Any analysis of the problem of the "in-between" states in Europe must begin with a clear definition of the term. The basic definition holds that in-between states are OSCE countries that are neither formally aligned with the "collective West" (i.e., the United States and EU) nor Russia. In other words, in-between states do not belong to NATO, the CSTO, the EU, or the EAEU. By this definition, nearly all European OSCE member states that are members of neither Western nor Russian alliances are in-between states.

But of course, not all of these states are of interest to this project, which examines the conflict between Russia and the West. We should restrict the definition to those states subject to the confrontation between the West and Russia—they are confronted with the issue of possible future membership in the geopolitical or geoeconomic alliances that embody the main geopolitical and geoeconomic centers on the European continent. States like Switzerland can thus be excluded given that there is a broader consensus between the West and Russia on their status.

Geographic location, specifically proximity to both blocs, plays a role here. For instance, Ukraine, Georgia, Azerbaijan, and Moldova are located in a space that physically divides Russia and the West. Others, like Serbia, Macedonia, and Bosnia and Herzegovina, are geopolitically and geoeconomically but not physically caught between Russia and the West, as they do not share borders with Russia. They can be thought of as geopolitical and geoeconomic enclaves within NATO and the EU. Many in the West consider their eventual membership in Euro-Atlantic institutions inevitable, but clearly Russia seems to be contesting that.

That said, the evidence suggests that geographical location has a crucial impact on the level and intensity of competition between the West and Russia. This conclusion is substantiated by the fact that today all the states physically located in between the West and Russia—Ukraine, Georgia, Moldova, and Azerbaijan—are suffering from hot or frozen conflicts.

Some experts, including some participants in this project, include Belarus and Armenia in their definition of in-between states. They argue that these states are increasingly becoming objects of geopolitical competition between the West and Russia in the past several years. However, both states have formally defined their geopolitical and geoeconomic status after having joined as full members of both the CSTO and the EAEU. Nonetheless, some Western diplomats and experts do not exclude, especially after 2014, the possibility of their geopolitical re-orientation and therefore pursue certain activities to this end.[1] Under conditions of growing confrontation between the West and Russia, triggered by the Ukraine crisis, such an approach could further destabilize European security. If Belarus and Armenia are considered in-between states, so too should EU and NATO member states like Hungary and Latvia, where some Russian experts consider geopolitical re-orientation possible. In short, if we are consistent about the criteria, only Ukraine, Moldova, Georgia, and Azerbaijan count as in-between states.

The Case of Ukraine as an In-Between

To understand possible security and political arrangements for in-between states, Ukraine offers an important case for analysis. Because of its economic and military potential, and strategic geographic location, Ukraine has been at the center of conflict between the West and Russia since its independence. After all, it was Russia's illegal annexation of Crimea and war in eastern Ukraine that called into question the basic principles of the post–Cold War European order. Therefore, identifying possible ways forward for Ukraine, or at least sustainable de-escalation of the crisis, has implications far beyond Ukraine and should be a priority.[2]

Ukraine's Security Status: A Historical Overview
1991–1996: The Road Not Taken to Permanent Neutrality
When Ukraine declared its independence on August 24, 1991, Kyiv was officially striving to become a permanently neutral state. This intention was codified in the Ukrainian parliament's declaration of independence from the Soviet Union, adopted on July 16, 1990.[3] The declaration stated the country's intention to become a permanently neutral state that would not participate in any military blocs and would follow the three of principles of a non-nuclear weapons state: to neither possess, produce, nor acquire nuclear weapons. Likewise, the country's first Law on Defense, which entered into force on December 6, 1991, reaffirmed that Ukraine was striving towards neutrality and adherence to the three non-nuclear principles.[4]

It is important to underscore that Ukraine's neutrality was historically linked with its abdication of the nuclear arsenal Kyiv inherited from the Soviet Union. It is therefore not accidental that the 1994 Budapest Memorandum, which formalized Ukraine's accession to the Nuclear Non-Proliferation Treaty (NPT), was linked with assurances of Ukraine's security and territorial integrity from the permanent members of the UN Security Council, including the United States and Russia.[5] In other words, the Budapest Memorandum was, in essence, a particular form of international recognition of the status of Ukraine as a neutral state, because it implies

---

[1] See, for example, Nelli Babayan, *The In-Betweeners: The Eastern Partnership Countries and the Russia-West Conflict*, Transatlantic Academy, 2015–2016 Paper Series, No. 5, April 2016, p. 13.

[2] Having directly participated in the development and adoption of all key international agreements related to the international security of Ukraine between 1993–2009, I have a clear understanding of many issues related to the crisis and crucial elements of possible viable and sustainable arrangements to restore security in this region.

[3] Verkhovna Rada, Deklaratsiya pro derzhavnyi suverenitet Ukrayiny, Kyiv, July 16, 1990.

[4] Verkhovna Rada, Pro zbroini Syly Ukrayiny, Kyiv, 1992.

[5] United Nations Security Council, Memorandum on Security Assurances in Connection with Ukraine's Accession to the Treaty on the Non-Proliferation of Nuclear Weapons, New York, December 19, 1994.

that for issues related to its national security, Ukraine must not take the side of one of its guarantors against the interests of another. From this perspective, the Budapest Memorandum is similar to the 1955 Austrian State Treaty, in which the Soviet Union, United States, United Kingdom, and France guaranteed Austria's status as an independent and permanent neutral state, although the Austrian State Treaty was much more explicit about the country's neutral status.

After signing the Budapest Memorandum, Ukraine could have further strengthened its status as a permanently neutral state by both following the principles of neutrality in its foreign policy de facto and by seeking international legal recognition of its neutral status by other states and international organizations. Unfortunately, history did not unfold this way. Immediately after the memorandum signing, Ukraine's foreign policy began to retreat from neutrality.

1996–2010: Route to Integration/Membership of Ukraine in NATO

Starting in 1996, Ukraine's integration with NATO was established as the country's official policy. In 1997, Ukraine's relations with NATO were formalized and plans for comprehensive cooperation hatched. For example, Ukraine signed the Charter on a Distinctive Partnership between NATO and Ukraine on July 9, 1997, at a summit in Madrid, which established the NATO-Ukraine Council.[6] In the early 2000s, Ukraine officially declared its objective of eventually becoming a member of NATO. For example, on May 23, 2002, Ukraine's National Security and Defense Council, which is chaired by the president, declared the country's intention to join NATO.[7] On April 6, 2004, the parliament adopted a status of forces agreement, allowing NATO forces to operate on the territory of Ukraine.[8]

Ukraine's aspirations for NATO membership reached their peak on April 3, 2008, at the NATO summit in Bucharest. Kyiv hoped the summit would kick off its Membership Action Plan process, which involves taking concrete steps toward accession to NATO. NATO members could not reach consensus on this step, but instead issued a declaration stating, "We agreed today that [Ukraine and Georgia] will become members of NATO."[9] However, no practical steps to achieve this outcome were proposed, nor was a timeline for accession made clear. In practice, this development indefinitely postponed the clarification of Ukraine's geopolitical alignment (or nonalignment) and reinforced its status as an in-between state—a reality that has created serious challenges for Ukraine.

2010–2014: Non-Bloc Policy

After Yanukovych came to power in 2010, the pace of cooperation with NATO slowed, and Ukraine's aim of membership was removed from the country's official foreign policy. Instead, a new law on foreign policy declared Ukraine's "non-bloc status."[10] Article 11 of the law defined Ukraine as a non-bloc state that would not participate in military-political alliances. However, the law did not provide certainty regarding Ukraine's geopolitical status. The Ukrainian elite was

---

[6]   NATO, Charter on a Distinctive Partnership Between the North Atlantic Treaty Organization and Ukraine, Madrid, July 9, 1997.

[7]   Verkhovna Rada, Pro stratehiyu Ukrayiny shchodo Orhanizatsiyi Pivnichnoatlantychnoho Dohovoru (NATO), Kyiv, May 23, 2002.

[8]   Radio Svoboda, "Prezident Ukrainy Leonid Kuchma pidpysav Zakon Pro shvidkyi dostup viisk' NATO na Ukrayins'ku teritoriyu," April 6, 2004.

[9]   NATO, 2008.

[10]   Verkhovna Rada, Pro zasady vnutrishn'oyi i zovnishn'oyi polityky, Kyiv, July 1, 2010.

not prepared to rule out any options permanently, and maintained a degree of ambiguity about the meaning of "non-bloc status." As Yanukovych's foreign minister wrote at the time, for him, "non-bloc status" meant that Ukraine was "open, not closed, for cooperation with NATO."[11] The ambiguity surrounding this issue—and the sense of the outside powers that it could easily change with a new government—contributed to the crisis in and around Ukraine that began in 2014.

Since 2014: Route to NATO Membership Again

After the February 2014 Maidan Revolution and Petro Poroshenko's rise to power as president of Ukraine in May that year, Ukraine's non-bloc status was revoked and NATO membership once again became a priority of Ukrainian foreign policy. On December 23, 2014, the parliament formalized these changes in amendments to the law "On principles of National Security of Ukraine" and the law "On principles of domestic and foreign policy."[12] These amendments reaffirm Ukraine's desire to pursue Euro-Atlantic integration and establish Ukraine's goal of deepening of cooperation with NATO in order to meet its membership criteria. These are the country's current primary foreign policy objectives.

Conclusions

Ukraine has existed as an in-between state for the last 26 years. Its foreign policy has been defined by a chaotic and unsustainable attempt at balancing between the West and Russia. As a result, Ukraine has found itself in a security vacuum, it has lost control over some of its own territory, and is forced to exercise its right to self-defense against Russian aggression on its own. Ukraine has transformed from a state that, in the late 1990s and early 2000s, was almost universally acknowledged as a key element in the emerging European security system to the main source of instability in Europe. Given Ukraine's integral role in European security, any restoration of sustainable peace and security in the region seems impossible without finding a solution to the crisis.

All parties, including Ukraine, Russia, and the West, should acknowledge responsibility for the security crisis in and around Ukraine. The West and Russia should take responsibility for not reaching a consensus on a mutually acceptable security arrangement for Ukraine. Ukraine should recognize that by taking varying sides in the confrontation between the West and Russia since 1991, especially on issues of great strategic importance, it too bears some responsibility for its own predicament.

Possible Future Scenarios for Ukraine

There are five possible scenarios that could emerge from the current crisis in and around Ukraine. I characterize these as war, peace, neither war nor peace, cold war, and cold peace. The first two scenarios listed—all-out war or complete peace—seem highly improbable given current conditions, so they will not be considered here. Of the three that are considered, neither war nor peace (Scenario 1) is essentially the status quo, whereas cold war (Scenario 2) and cold peace (Scenario 3) could be implemented in the future.

---

[11] Konstantin Grishchenko, "Za predelami shakhmatnoi doski: pragmatichnaya povestka dnya Ukrainskoi vneshnei politiki," *Zerkalo nedeli*, July 16, 2010.

[12] Verkhovna Rada, Pro vnesennya zmin do deyakyh zakoniv Ukrayiny shchodo vidmovy Ukrayiny vid zdiysnennya polityky pozablokovosti, Kyiv, December 23, 2014.

Scenario 1: Neither War Nor Peace

In this scenario, that is, status quo conditions, Ukraine's alignment remains undetermined and fierce competition between the West and Russia over Ukraine without agreed rules of the game will continue. The West will continue to highlight Ukraine's right under the Helsinki Principles to choose its security alliances freely, while Russia will point to the dueling Helsinki Principle of indivisibility of security.[13] Neither side wants to limit its future freedom of maneuver by establishing any clear rules or agreed security arrangements, except in urgent cases, such as the Minsk Agreements. These accords are designed to end the fighting in eastern Ukraine rather than to create a sustainable peaceful settlement of the crisis in and around Ukraine. However, the past three years have demonstrated that a sustainable ceasefire is impossible without a comprehensive settlement that creates mutually acceptable security arrangements for Ukraine. Under this scenario, such a solution is not possible, and therefore the crisis in and around Ukraine continues to unfold in the form of a low intensity military confrontation. The resulting strategic ambiguity would be extremely dangerous for Ukraine's security and territorial integrity because it leaves Kyiv to defend against Russian aggression in eastern Ukraine by itself. In this scenario, Ukraine is left without any formal guarantees from the West to provide real assistance in the framework of collective defense in case of a full-scale Russian invasion.

Scenario 2: Cold War

The cold war scenario would obtain if the West and Russia were prepared to establish specific red lines and find mutually acceptable security arrangements, which would limit—not end—their confrontation over Ukraine. Specifically, the West and Russia would have to agree to a deep freeze of the conflict in Donbas, beginning with a sustainable ceasefire at the current line of contact, and eventually a peacekeeping operation to enforce it.

In this scenario, Ukraine would be similar to West Germany in the Cold War. Ukraine, the West, and Russia (without prejudice for Ukraine's sovereignty over Donbas and Crimea) would undertake obligations not to use force to change the de facto existing contact lines with both Donbas and Crimea. Although it would not be guaranteed, Kyiv would hope that it would eventually regain its territorial integrity, as Germany did in 1989.

In the framework of the cold war scenario, Ukraine could join NATO (as West Germany did) as a part of package agreement between the West and Russia, involving, for example, lifting the sanctions against Russia. Alternatively, the United States could designate Ukraine a major non-NATO ally.

In this scenario, the West and Russia (as in the Cold War) would not cease their competition over Ukraine. Instead, their competition would follow agreed-upon rules. This is the crucial difference between this scenario and scenario 1 above.

Scenario 3: Cold Peace

The cold peace scenario assumes that both the West and Russia attempt to resolve the security crisis in and around Ukraine on the basis of cooperation, not confrontation. This scenario acknowledges the need to reach a long-term and sustainable strategic consensus among Ukraine, the West, and Russia regarding the status of Ukraine as an in-between state. It is

---

[13] Organization for Security and Co-operation in Europe, Conference on Security and Cooperation in Europe Final Act, Helsinki, August 1, 1975.

clear that this scenario requires the most diplomatic effort and political will from all actors involved, including Ukraine.

In the framework of this scenario, Ukraine, the West, and Russia can choose among several options for mutually acceptable security arrangements involving Ukraine.

- First, they could declare Ukraine's neutral status on the basis of legally binding security arrangements and guarantees. It would mean some kind of "Austrianization" of Ukraine using the framework adopted in the 1955 Austrian State Treaty. This treaty restored Austria as independent and democratic, and its signatories—the Soviet Union, United States, United Kingdom, and France—guaranteed Austria's status as a permanently neutral state.
- A second option would be to implement a similar framework by transforming the Budapest Memorandum into a legally binding document through a UN Security Council resolution.
- Third, a special international legal agreement could be developed in which the West and Russia formally acknowledge Ukraine's status as a permanently neutral state.
- A fourth approach would involve codifying Ukraine's neutrality through non–legally binding commitments by a simple reconfirmation of the security assurances contained in the Budapest Memorandum by the signatories of that document.
- Lastly, this could be achieved through the international acknowledgement of Ukraine's nonaligned status on the basis of a constitutional amendment enacted domestically. This approach would mirror that of Finland after World War II.

Given Ukraine's post-Soviet history described above, the Austrian framework seems most likely to succeed in this case because it involves all parties' agreeing to the same principles and rules of the road.

Moving from Confrontation to Cooperation Regarding the States In Between

To bring about the most positive scenario for Ukraine, the West and Russia would have to begin to move from confrontation to cooperation in their approach not only to Ukraine but also to the other in-between states. This confrontation was the main cause of the current deep systemic crisis in the relations between the West and Russia. As the result of that crisis, the European security order has been broken, and the overall interaction between Russia and the West is characterized by steadily increasing tensions. We can assume that these tensions between Russia and the West in Europe will continue to mount.

Today it is evident that the problem of the states in between has triggered the start of a new cold war in Europe. A large package of principles, norms and ad hoc policies will be needed to solve the problem. Only such an approach would make it possible to turn from confrontation to cooperation between the West and Russia regarding the states in between. The approach requires measures at three levels:

1. the Great Powers (West and Russia)
2. states in between
3. OSCE and Council of Europe.

The Great Powers

Without political will from the West and Russia, it is not possible to stop their confrontation regarding the strategic choices of the in-between states. A new détente should begin the process of building a consensus between the West and Russia regarding the status of the in-between states. The basis for such a consensus should be an acknowledgement that NATO and the EU, on the one hand, and the CSTO and the EAEU, on the other, have reached their natural geographical limits. Attempts to continue enlarging them unilaterally, that is, without Great Power consensus, will profoundly destabilize European security in all its aspects.

In other words, further unilateral enlargement of these institutions to include other in-between states is no longer possible without putting at stake their territorial integrity and sovereignty, two of the main principles of the Helsinki Final Act. Therefore, the West and Russia should undertake an obligation that any new enlargement of either side's institutions would only be possible on the basis of clear mutual consent of both sides.

To reach and implement such a consensus, the West and Russia should reconfirm the inter-relationship, as stipulated in the Paris Charter and the OSCE Astana Declaration, between the principle of freedom of choice to join alliances and the principle of indivisibility of security—i.e., the security of one state is inextricably linked to the security of all.[14] Such a move would be consistent with NATO membership criteria, which state that all prospective members should settle their territorial and border disputes with their neighbors before joining.[15]

As a next step, the West and Russia, together with all the states in between, should immediately start a comprehensive discussion in the framework of the OSCE to agree on a geopolitical and geoeconomic status for the in-betweens that would be acceptable for parties. Decisions on specific in-between states' security arrangements should be taken on the basis of consensus. But we can expect that any agreement reached through such negotiations could include the following elements:

- a Treaty on European security
- alliance membership or military assistance outside an alliance framework
- permanent or time-limited neutrality
- neutrality but with military links with NATO and/or the CSTO
- multilateral security guarantees.

To begin this process, Russia and the West could either jointly put forward an idea to conduct a pan-OSCE summit on European security (something like a "Helsinki 2.0") where the problem of the states in between would be resolved as one of the main priorities or they could initiate separate summits with each state in between on its security status with the involvement of all interested OSCE states.

The States In Between

Under conditions of increased confrontation between the West and Russia, the states in between should apply the best practices of states like Austria and Finland, which allowed those states not only to prevent their countries from becoming the locus of a great power clash but also to contribute to great power peace. The in-between states must recognize that their choices

---

[14] OSCE, 1990; OSCE, *Astana Commemorative Declaration Towards a Security Community*, Astana, December 1, 2010.

[15] NATO, *Study on NATO Enlargement*, Brussels, September 3, 1995.

have contributed to the increase of tensions between the West and Russia and have, in some cases, threatened their own territorial integrity and statehood. Even if the West and Russia cannot reach consensus on their geopolitical and geoeconomic status, the in-between states can and should undertake obligations to conduct their own foreign and security policies on the basis of the principles of neutrality or nonalignment. In other words, they should maintain equal distance from both Russia and the West.

The history of the last 25 years has demonstrated the truth of a simple rule: If a state in between wants to enter a geopolitical or geoeconomic alliance with either side when the great powers do not have consensus about the issue, then such a state will be partitioned. The only question is how, where, or when the partitioning would happen (see the examples of Moldova, Georgia, and Ukraine). While all of the separatist entities in these countries at least in part grew out of genuine grievances of local populations, these grievances—and the resulting territorial disputes—have since been instrumentalized for geopolitical purposes. During the Cold War, states physically in between the two blocs that conducted a policy of neutrality preserved their territorial integrity even though great power tensions were high (e.g., Austria and Finland). The in-between states should also recognize that a new détente between the West and Russia is the best basis for a peaceful negotiation process to restore their territorial integrity and resolve the conflicts in their countries.

The OSCE and the Council of Europe

In accordance with their statutory powers, the OSCE and the Council of Europe should do everything possible to include on their agenda the issues that would contribute to implementation of proposals mentioned above. They should also restart the processes of a new détente and drafting of respective new policies to reach a sustainable consensus between the West and Russia over the geopolitical and geoeconomic status of the in-between states.

CHAPTER SIX

Cooperative Transregionalism and the Problem of the "In Betweens"

Yulia Nikitina, Ph.D.
Associate Professor of World Politics
Moscow State Institute of International Relations

Russian-Western relations are currently in a crisis, which has cast a shadow on the so-called in-between countries as well. The paradox is that from the West's perspective, the crisis in relations with Russia started unexpectedly in 2014 with Moscow's activities in Ukraine. Russia, by contrast, believes the crisis to have originated in patterns that began as early as the Kosovo conflict in 1999. For the West, the crisis is regional and is about European/Eurasian security, while for Russia the crisis is global and is about the rules of the world order and norms of interference in domestic affairs. Thus, while a solution designed to address regional security issues in Europe/Eurasia might be more beneficial from the Western perspective, it will not fully end the clash for Moscow, which aspires to set the rules not only regionally, but also at the global level.

Russia believes that "powerful regional organizations" should be at the center of global governance, and that international stability will be assured if rules of interaction of regional organizations are developed.[1] The present paper develops this idea about interorganizational dialogue as a means to undergird global and regional security and explains why such cooperation might be beneficial for Western institutions as well.

Currently, the West essentially refuses to recognize the Russia-led regional organizations—the CSTO and the EAEU—which has caused a deadlock in interorganizational interaction. Without such recognition, dialogue to iron out differences is impossible. This paper proposes a solution to this deadlock that would foster practical interaction between organizations but avoids the recognition question entirely. While it will not solve all existing issues, greater institutional dialogue—leading to cooperative transregionalism—could alleviate the pressure on the in-between states and prevent them from having to make binary choices.

Regional Integration as a Means to Prevent New Conflicts

Conceptually, there can be opposing strategies for preventing the repetition of a conflict: (1) isolating a potentially dangerous actor (sanctions and exclusion from international forums),

---

[1] Official Internet Resources of the President of Russia, "Remarks at the Meeting of the Valdai International Discussion Club," October 24, 2014.

or (2) integrating this actor into wider regional structures to establish control over its capacity building. The experience of the two World Wars demonstrated that isolationism and exclusion leads to revanchism, while integration and transparency within institutions leads to peaceful coexistence. However, the cases of post-World War II Germany and Japan can be explained not only by the inclusion of two countries into the Western democratic world, but also by regime change and occupation.

These cases raise the question of whether integration can be achieved without prior regime change and external democratization involving institution-building and reforms. Further, do all three elements—regime change, democratization (homegrown or imported), and integration—need to be combined for successful integration? The sequencing is another important issue. Do regime change and democratization facilitate integration, or conversely, does integration lead to further democratization of domestic institutions and, finally, to peaceful change of regime?

It seems that the West and Russia have the opposite view on the optimal sequence of these stages. From the Western perspective, integration into Euro-Atlantic institutions is a reward. For Russia, integration is a starting point for reforms, which might eventually lead to the country's increased competitiveness in global affairs. For Russia, integration is a mechanism for the socialization of states into a wider regional and even global community.

Russian and Western approaches to inter-organizational cooperation differ as well. For the EU and NATO, interorganizational cooperation can be viable only after a potential partner has demonstrated a certain degree of effectiveness, sustainability, and real achievements. Thus, the CSTO and the EAEU are not seen as attractive partners, because of their perceived lack of effectiveness and questionable sustainability. Conversely, for the CSTO and the EAEU, interorganizational ties would increase their capacity through socialization within a wider region. Thus, for the CSTO and the EAEU, the content of interorganizational cooperation is not as important compared to the fact of cooperation itself.

Additionally, Russia and the West have different recipes for using institutions to foster stability and prosperity. For Russia, social stability and prosperity are prerequisites for successful regional institution building and even the development of civil society and democratic practices. For the West, by contrast, the ascension of civil society and democratization derives from the process of regional institution-building, and further prosperity and stabilization is achieved on the basis of these institutions. Thus, European "transformative regionalism" aimed at region-building on the EU borders (as embodied in the Eastern Partnership program for the six countries in between) is based on the assumption that European norms and institutions provide stability and prosperity.[2]

A possible compromise between Russia and the West in order to create more solid foundations for stability and prosperity for the in-between states, and for Eurasia in general, will have to deal with different Russian and Western approaches to these phenomena. Particularly since this divergence in approaches is at the core of the political clash over the EU's AAs with the in-between states, which was the spark of the Ukraine crisis in 2014.

One possible solution would be to reframe once again the relationship between the two institutional centers of gravity as cooperative rather than competitive. Hypothetically, the scheme of Eurasian continent-wide regional integration depicted in Figure 6.1 would allow for greater cooperation, rather than conflict, between centers of influence.

---

[2] Thomas Diez and Michelle Pace, "Normative Power Europe and Conflict Transformation," paper presented at the 2007 European Union Studies Association Conference, Montreal, May 17–19, 2007.

Figure 6.1
Model of Norm Diffusion Through Regional Integration

RAND *CF382-6.1*

In this scheme, Russia would act as an agent of regional transformation by transfer of Euro-Atlantic norms to other countries in the region. The competition in this scheme is not so evident, because every actor gets what it wants: The West is able to promote its values, Russia acts as a modernization role model and regional leader, and in-between states get a clear model of development adapted to the local conditions.

In fact, this model has organically emerged in the case of the EAEU, which has adopted many norms and standards from the EU. Unlike in the framework proposed here, however, the EU does not formally participate in this norm transfer and adaptation. In practice, the proposed approach is unlikely to be implemented for clear political reasons; it is unacceptable to many of Russia's neighbors. But it should be maintained as one option for the future if political circumstances were to change.

Cooperative Transregionalism

Since such a cooperative top-down norms transfer is highly unlikely, designing a macro-strategy for cooperation that would include different regional development models under an umbrella of a common denominator could be a potential solution.

The current Russian strategy of finding such a common denominator can be called *"cooperative transregionalism."* This concept is developed at two levels: global and pan-European.

At the global level, for a number of years Russia has endorsed the idea that "powerful regional organizations," rather than individual great powers, may constitute future global centers of influence. In 2014, in his Valdai speech, Putin formulated this message rather clearly:

> Cooperation between these centers would seriously add to the stability of global security, policy and economy. But in order to establish such a dialogue, we need to proceed from the assumption that all regional centers and integration projects forming around them need to have equal rights to development, so that they can complement each other and nobody can force them into conflict or opposition artificially.[3]

In September 2015, Putin presented the idea of "integration of integrations" at the UN General Assembly session: "Contrary to the policy of exclusion, Russia advocates harmonizing regional economic projects. I am referring to the so-called 'integration of integrations' based

---

[3] Official Internet Resources of the President of Russia, 2014.

on the universal and transparent rules of international trade."[4] The chosen venue for promotion of the concept suggests that this idea has a global reach rather than just a Eurasian regional scope. The concept of "integration of integrations" is a new edition of ideas promoted in the proposal for a European Security Treaty, put forward by Russia in 2008.[5] The 2008 proposal covered regional security, while more recent Russian projects deal with economic integration.

Transregional Network of Institutions

In order to avoid the "integration dilemma" of choosing between European/Euro-Atlantic integration and Eurasian integration, a cooperative trans-regionalism strategy in the format of a *transregional network of institutions and projects* might offer a solution.[6] Although the EU and NATO claim that there is no competition and no integration dilemma and note the right for in-between countries to make independent foreign policy choices, from the Russian perspective and the perspective of the countries in between, such a competition exists.

The Russian concept of integration of integrations is currently manifest in the so called Greater Eurasia project.[7] The Greater Eurasia project, as Russia conceives it, should be based on the cooperation among the EAEU, the Shanghai Cooperation Organization (SCO), Association of Southeast Asian Nations (ASEAN), and China's Belt and Road Initiative (BRI). The basis for this future cooperation should be open regionalism based on WTO principles with a long-term goal of creating a free-trade area among the mentioned organizations and projects. This idea was endorsed in principle by Russia and ASEAN member states at a summit in Sochi in May 2016, where a meeting of the representatives of the secretariats of the EAEU, SCO, and ASEAN took place.

If the Greater Eurasia project proves successful, it might create a basis for a supra-regional identity on the basis of open regionalism where competing regional projects first settle the integration dilemmas so that "in-between" countries would not have to choose between different centers of influence. In order to achieve this objective, however, the EU would have to join the project, and such a step seems highly unlikely at this stage.

A Tale of Two Blocs: NATO and the CSTO

For the time being, the best chance at cooperation is for the existing organizations to have some sort of interaction with each other. Unfortunately, even on this level there has been little success. Since 2004, the CSTO has made several attempts to establish interorganizational relations with NATO. From the NATO perspective, such an official recognition of the CSTO would be counterproductive, because in their eyes Russia initiated the CSTO to counter NATO and U.S. influence, and any NATO-CSTO engagement would only increase Russian influence over Central Asia.[8] NATO has stated this position in its official communications. For instance, according to former NATO Secretary General Rasmussen in 2012,

---

[4]   Official Internet Resources of the President of Russia, "Remarks at the 70th Session of the UN General Assembly," September 28, 2015.

[5]   Official Internet Resources of the President of Russia, "European Security Treaty," November 29, 2009.

[6]   Samuel Charap and Mikhail Troitskiy, "Russia, the West and the Integration Dilemma," *Survival*, Vol. 55, No. 6, 2013, pp. 49–62.

[7]   Official Internet Resources of the President of Russia, "Remarks at the Belt and Road International Forum," May 14, 2017.

[8]   Joshua Kucera, "U.S. Blocking NATO-CSTO Cooperation," EURASIANET.org, February 12, 2011.

"we cooperate with individual nations. We don't think it's necessary to build new institutional structures between NATO and CSTO as an organization."[9] Yet, despite NATO's position and soured relations between Russia and the West, in 2017 the CSTO expressed regret at the lack of interaction with NATO.[10]

Political disagreements aside, what could be the practical approaches to potential NATO-CSTO cooperation? The CSTO representatives over the last ten years named different possible areas of cooperation, summarized in Table 6.1.

In 2007, the CSTO sought to cooperate with NATO on some hard security issues like weapons of mass destruction issues and export controls despite the fact that these issues are not top priorities for the CSTO in that it only adopts political declarations on them. Such suggestions for cooperation on hard security could suggest that the CSTO perceived NATO as more of a classical military bloc, or it could also mean that Russia as a nuclear state and large arms exporter was the main agenda-setter within the CSTO. However, all of these issues are already subject areas of NATO-Russia or U.S.-Russia relations, so there is no need to create another platform for discussing them, particularly because among CSTO members only Russia can support a substantive dialogue on hard security. In 2012, hard security issues disappeared from the agenda of the CSTO's proposed areas for cooperation with NATO.

Afghanistan has remained the top priority in the list of CSTO suggestions for areas of inter-organizational cooperation with NATO. However, from the very beginning of the operation in Afghanistan, NATO and the U.S. established bilateral cooperation with Russia and Central Asian states over the issues related to this operation. With the formal end of the NATO International Security Assistance Force mission in 2014, it is very difficult to find any new reasons to establish NATO-CSTO cooperation over Afghan security.

Recommendations

Perhaps Russia and the West could learn from the experience of the SCO, a club with membership of very large and very small countries with different regimes, cultures, religions, and histories. The SCO adopted the so-called Shanghai spirit to achieve progress: Members are ready to spend as much time as needed on negotiations to reach consensus. There is no outright veto in the SCO, and the organizational culture implies that an issue may stay on the agenda until a solution is found.[11] From the Western perspective, these characteristics of organizational procedure are seen as very slow, ineffective, and counterproductive, while for the SCO they are just part of its organizational philosophy.

The Shanghai spirit could be relevant for beginning the process of transregional, Russia-West cooperation in Eurasia. This implies long-term negotiations without viewing lack of consensus as a stalemate or an obstacle to further consultations. This approach offers a middle-of-the-road solution to the problem of interorganizational cooperation between Eurasian institutions, on the one hand, and Western institutions on the other. Specifically, the sides

---

[9] NATO, "Press Conference by NATO Secretary General Anders Fogh Rasmussen with Moscow-Based Journalists," March 26, 2012.

[10] "V ODKB Ukazali na Otsutstvie Sotrudnichestva s NATO," *Voennoe Obozrenie*, April 25, 2017.

[11] I.E. Denisov and I.A. Safranchuk, "Four Problems of the SCO in Connection with its Enlargement," *Russian Politics and Law*, Vol. 54, No. 5–6, 2016, pp. 494–515.

Table 6.1
The CSTO's Views on Areas of Possible Cooperation Between the CSTO and NATO

Year	Areas of Possible Cooperation
2007[a]	Counterterrorism and drug trafficking Nonproliferation of weapons of mass destruction Export controls Post-conflict assistance to Afghanistan Border management
2009[b]	Afghanistan: joint anti-drug-trafficking operations in Afghanistan plus assistance in creating national anti-drug-trafficking legislation in Afghanistan, training and equipping Afghan security forces, economic assistance, organization of trans-border cooperation, civil and military transit
2012[c]	Fight against international terrorism and drug trafficking Restoring stability in Afghanistan; preventing threats from its territory; securing transit for ISAF needs; training and equipping Afghan security forces Joint reaction to man-made and natural disasters Mutual assistance in cases of evacuation of official diplomatic missions and citizens of CSTO and NATO countries in crisis situations Exchange of information about main aspects of CSTO and NATO activities
2013[d]	Joint efforts to stabilize Afghanistan and neutralize threats from Afghan territory Regular exchange of information about political and military developments in conflict-prone regions, discussion of possible joint steps Elaboration and implementation of coordinated measures to counter illegal drug trafficking, extremism and terrorism and to provide information security[e] Planning of coordinated steps to eliminate consequences of man-made or natural accidents or disasters Creation of a mechanism of joint discussion of the CSTO and of NATO's conceptual approaches to security Exchange of information between the CSTO and NATO about their collective rapid reaction forces Peacekeeping
2015[f]	Global security threats, which both NATO and the CSTO encounter

NOTE: This table and some conclusions in this part of the paper are partially based on the policy memo: Yulia Nikitina, "How the CSTO Can (and Cannot) Help NATO," *PONARS Eurasia*, Policy Memo 285, September 2013.

[a] Novosti-Armenia, "Armenia Is a Reliable, Time-Tested Partner in the System of Alliance Relations Among the CSTO Member-States," January 18, 2007.

[b] Voice of America, "The CSTO Invites NATO to Cooperate," December 15, 2009.

[c] RIA Novosti, "Council of the CSTO Foreign Affairs Ministers Adopted a Declaration about Cooperation with NATO," June 4, 2012.

[d] "CSTO Is Ready to Cooperate with NATO," *Rossiiskaya Gazeta*, May 23, 2013.

[e] In Russia, "information security" is not equivalent to "cyber security." The term "information security" is mostly used in relation to information warfare or extremist information on the web.

[f] "NATO Disregards the CSTO Suggestions About Cooperation—Bordyuzha," *Kazpravda.kz*, April 4, 2015.

could initiate a process of interorganizational consultations at the working group level to discuss and identify the potential areas for concrete cooperation. This format would satisfy Eurasian institutions because it offers them a platform for expressing their concerns. At the same time, it would not cross Western red lines, because they will not establish official relations with their counterparts (no recognition). Western officials would have the opportunity to demonstrate during the working discussions that that Eurasian institutions actually do not have any real agenda for interorganizational cooperation, if that is in fact the case.

Working groups could be organized according to the logic of specialization of organizations: EU-EAEU; NATO-CSTO; EU-EAEU-SCO-BRI (in the economic dimension); and OSCE-SCO (in the security dimension). The OSCE can be a third partner in EU-EAEU and

NATO-CSTO contacts as an organization with guiding principles of regional interaction. The OSCE may actually initiate such working groups within the OSCE itself.

One potential example agenda item for such groups could be NATO-CSTO cooperation on responses to natural and manmade disasters. This type of cooperation is politically neutral and involves working-level officials only.

NATO and CSTO could also partner on postconflict reconstruction and peace-building issues. The CSTO does not have a mandate to intervene in out-of-area conflicts, but it can join in at later stages of reconstruction and state-building.

There are greater incentives for Russia to find practical ways of coordinating and cooperating on this issue since it has been actively involved in military actions against the Islamic State in Syria, unlike in Afghanistan, where it did not have "boots on the ground." The CSTO is not involved in Russia's military operation in Syria and will not be in the picture, but postconflict peace-building and reconstruction may create a new opportunity for cooperation. In the first half of 2017, Russia opened consultations with its CSTO partners, Kazakhstan and Kyrgyzstan, about the potential of sending representatives of their military police services to serve as observers in the de-escalation zones in Syria.[12] Once the fighting is over, the CSTO might consider participating in postconflict reconstruction and peace-building, which could involve cooperation with NATO countries. This would depend on the role that NATO or individual member-states will have in postconflict reconstruction. Since Georgia and Ukraine are often active in NATO-led or U.S.-led operations abroad to demonstrate their readiness for future membership, joint postconflict reconstruction teams could include representatives of NATO allies, CSTO member states, and in-between countries.

Preventing radicalization of populations using social media is another possible arena for interaction. Unlike postconflict reconstruction and peace-building, which might be a less pressing area for cooperation, this issue is pressing both for NATO and the CSTO. Despite different approaches to cybersecurity, NATO and CSTO members share the understanding that the fight against international terrorism should be pursued both on the web and on the ground. Since 2009, the CSTO has conducted an annual exercise called "PROXY" aimed at shutting down the websites with extremist content enrolling terrorist fighters. Cooperation between Western and CSTO states could provide an opportunity to dispel any Western suspicions that political elites of the CSTO members use this operation to close down websites of their opponents. This would also be an opportunity to share best practices from the West's experience in identifying extremist content.

Conclusions

Cooperative transregionalism in the format of a network of regional economic and security organizations would serve as a solution for the "integration dilemma" for the in-between countries. This network will have to define the rules of interactions among different regional organizations to solve the problem of binary choices faced by the in-between states. However, in

---

[12] Kazakhstani and Kyrgyzstani representatives denied such consultations, and stated that their countries might be involved in the conflict settlement only if there is a UN mandate for such an operation. See "Russian Allies in the CSTO Do Not Want to Fight in Syria," *Nezavisimaya Gazeta*, June 26, 2017; RBC, "Russia Negotiated with Kazakhstan And Kyrgyzstan About Sending Their Troops to Syria," June 22, 2017.

the current political environment, this approach has little chance of success. A more modest short-term step could be interorganizational cooperation on a case-by-case basis. A specificity of these working groups might be their reliance on the Shanghai spirit of consensus building (no deadlock in case of disagreement, discussion continues until a common understanding is found) and no prior mutual recognition of organizations at the official level, just working contacts to study potential areas of cooperation and mutual concerns about this potential cooperation. The overall idea is to institutionalize competition between different regional organizations, much as it was done in 1975 with the Helsinki Final Act—ideological differences did not fundamentally impede the dialogue. The political and ideological conflict was transformed into structured discussions. The suggested interorganizational working groups would serve the same purpose.

Summary of Policy Recommendations

What follows is a brief summary, compiled by the volume editors, of the policy recommendations from each of the papers.

Dobbins and Zagorski

- A series of understandings and agreements involving most if not all OSCE members that would push any changes in the alignment of the former Soviet states into the distant future while creating a more favorable economic and security environment for these countries in the interim. Ultimately, such a set of arrangements should seek to reduce the pressures on the in-between states to seek membership in political-military alliances and, possibly, to make such membership unnecessary by increasing the benefits and incentives to pursue policies of nonalignment. This should not, however, prevent their closer economic integration and/or cooperation with both the EU or Russia/EAEU.
- These understandings and agreements could include:
  - Multilateral security guarantees: For example, the assurances from the 1994 Budapest Memorandum could be made legally binding through a UN Security Council Resolution.
  - Security benefits for countries that commit to nonaligned status, such as reliable assurances that their territory will not be used as a theater of hostilities between Russia and the West. In return, the relevant in-between states would need to pledge not to allow any permanent deployments of foreign combat forces, use of military infrastructure, or other hostile activities on their territory.
  - Arms control measures: a verifiable agreement committing all parties not to concentrate substantial combat forces on the borders of neutral or nonaligned states (the width of this effectively demilitarized area would be subject to negotiation) and not to conduct large-scale military exercises there. Any military activities of the parties below the level of large-scale exercises (as defined in the agreement) should be conducted in a transparent, verifiable, and cooperative manner.
  - Nonintervention in internal affairs: In order to address concerns pertaining to activities associated with hybrid conflict (measures short of conventional military hostilities), nonaligned countries in between should also receive assurances of non-intervention into their internal affairs.
  - Efforts should be undertaken to make EU DCFTAs and economic ties with the EAEU compatible.

– Committing to consult: creation of a forum in which all relevant parties would commit to pursue intensive and inclusive political consultations and dialogue on all issues that may arise from future developments.

Krumm

- For now, a grand bargain is very unlikely, so it makes sense to take small, well-defined steps.
- The first category of such steps are so-called islands of cooperation: joint work in a limited and small-scale area of cooperation. These should be issues of mutual interest, rather than those involving potential or real conflicts.
- Another category of small steps involves merely opening up dialogue on sensitive issues where interests clash. Such a dialogue should be structured and inclusive, with neutral observers monitoring progress.
- The EU and the EAEU could also initiate a separate structured dialogue. The aim would be to find common interests and begin working on concrete projects.
- Establishing bilateral CSBMs between Russia and individual in-between states, as envisaged in Chapter X of the 2011 Vienna Document, would be another relevant way forward.

Ademmer and Lissovolik

- Negotiate bilateral economic agreements among trade blocs and nonmembers in the region. The coexistence of various bilateral agreements would ideally interlock economies in a way that makes individual countries consider relationships with other trade blocs when enacting changes in their existing trade arrangements.
- Starting a more inclusive economic dialogue between the EU and the EAEU. As a first step, this could be designed as a simple diplomatic effort for basic information exchange on economic issues between the two organizations formally representing all members of the respective customs unions. If this approach is successful, it could serve as an organizational forum that might be extended to allow for trilateral consultations with additional partners in the region.
- Cooperation could also be enhanced between development institutions, such as the EBRD and the EDB, to support projects that may help to initiate specific forms of cooperation and further common economic goals, such as infrastructure development.

Chalyi

- The West and Russia have to begin to move from confrontation to cooperation in their approach not only to Ukraine, but also to the other in-between states. A large package of principles, norms, and ad hoc policies will be needed to solve the problem.
- The approach requires measures at three levels: the Great Powers, the in-between states, and the OSCE and Council of Europe.

- The basis for such a consensus should be an acknowledgement that both Euro-Atlantic institutions (NATO and the EU) and Eurasian institutions (the CSTO and the EAEU) have reached their respective natural geographical limits.
- The West and Russia, together with all the in-between states, should immediately start a comprehensive discussion in the framework of the OSCE to agree on a geopolitical and geoeconomic status for the in-betweens that would be acceptable for parties.
- Even if the West and Russia cannot reach consensus on their geopolitical and geoeconomic status, the states in between can and should undertake obligations to conduct their own foreign and security policies on the basis of the principles of neutrality or non-alignment. In other words, they should maintain equal distance from both Russia and the West.
- In accordance with their statutory powers, the OSCE and the Council of Europe should do everything possible to include on their agenda the issues that would contribute to implementation of proposals mentioned above. They should also restart the processes of a new détente and drafting of respective new policies to reach a sustainable consensus between the West and Russia over the geopolitical and geoeconomic status of the states in between.

Nikitina

- The "Shanghai spirit"—long-term negotiations without viewing lack of consensus as a stalemate or an obstacle to further consultations—should be adopted as a basis for Russia-West interorganizational dialogue.
  - Specifically, the sides could initiate a process of interorganizational consultations at the working group level to discuss and identify the potential areas for concrete cooperation. This format would satisfy Eurasian institutions because it offers them a platform for expressing their concerns. At the same time, it would not cross Western red lines, because they will not establish official relations with their counterparts (no recognition).
  - Working groups could be organized according to the logic of specialization of organizations: EU-EAEU, NATO-CSTO, EU-EAEU-SCO-BRI (in the economic dimension), and OSCE-SCO (in the security dimension). The OSCE can be a third partner in EU-EAEU and NATO-CSTO contacts as an organization with guiding principles of regional interaction. The OSCE may actually initiate such working groups within the OSCE itself.
- NATO and CSTO could partner on postconflict reconstruction and peace-building issues.
  - Once the fighting in Syria is over, the CSTO might consider participating in postconflict reconstruction and peace-building, which could involve cooperation with NATO countries.
  - Preventing radicalization of populations using social media is another possible arena for interaction.

References

Adarov, Amat, and Peter Havlik, "Benefits and Costs of DCFTA: Evaluation of the Impact on Georgia, Moldova, and Ukraine," Joint Working Paper of WIIW and Bertelsmann Stiftung, Vienna Institute for International Economic Studies, 2016.

Auswärtiges Amt, "Rede von Staatssekretär Markus Ederer beim Jahresempfang des Ost-Ausschusses der Deutschen Wirtschaft: 'Euraien-Brennpunkt der Interessen oder Raum der Kooperation?'" webpage, 2017. As of August 28, 2017:
http://www.auswaertiges-amt.de/DE/Infoservice/Presse/Reden/2017/170712_StS_E_Ostausschuss.html?searchArchive=0&searchEngineQueryString=Eurasische+Wirtschaftsunion&path=%2Fdiplo%2FDE*&searchIssued=0&searchIssuedAfter=27.11.2013

Babayan, Nelli, *The In-Betweeners: The Eastern Partnership Countries and the Russia-West Conflict*, Transatlantic Academy, 2015–2016 Paper Series, No. 5, April 2016, p. 13. As of December 7, 2017:
http://www.transatlanticacademy.org/sites/default/files/publications/Babayan_Inbetweeners_Apr16_web.pdf

Bruszt, László, and Julia Langbein, "Varieties of Dis-Embedded Liberalism: EU Integration Strategies in the Eastern Peripheries of Europe," *Journal of European Public Policy*, Vol. 24, No. 2, 2017, pp. 297–315.

Charap, Samuel, and Mikhail Troitskiy, "Russia, the West and the Integration Dilemma," *Survival*, Vol 55, No. 6, 2013, pp. 49–62. As of November 21, 2017:
https://doi.org/10.1080/00396338.2013.862935

Choi, Won-Mog, "Legal Problems of Making Regional Trade Agreements With Non-WTO-Member States," *Journal of International Economic Law*, Vol. 8, No. 4, 2005, pp. 825–860.

Connolly, Richard, "Russia, the Eurasian Customs Union and the WTO," in Rilka Dragneva and Kataryna Wolczuk, eds., *Eurasian Economic Integration: Law, Policy and Politics*, Cheltenham: Edward Elgar, 2013, pp. 61–78.

Crozet, Matthieu, and Julian Hinz, *Collateral Damage: The Impact of The Russia Sanctions on Sanctioning Countries' Exports*, CEPII Working Paper, Vol. 59, 2016. As of November 14, 2017:
http://www.cepii.fr/PDF_PUB/wp/2016/wp2016-16.pdf

"CSTO Is Ready to Cooperate with NATO," *Rossiiskaya Gazeta*, May 23, 2013. As of November 20, 2017:
http://www.rg.ru/2013/05/23/odkb-site.html

Deep Cuts Commission, *Back from the Brink: Toward Restraint and Dialogue Between Russia and the West*, Institute for Peace Research and Security Policy at the University of Hamburg, June 2016. As of November 29, 2017:
http://www.deepcuts.org/images/PDF/Third_Report_of_the_Deep_Cuts_Commission_English.pdf

Denisov, I. E. and I. A. Safranchuk, "Four Problems of the SCO in Connection with Its Enlargement," *Russian Politics and Law*, Vol. 54, No. 5–6, 2016, pp. 494–515.

Diez, Thomas, and Michelle Pace, "Normative Power Europe and Conflict Transformation," paper presented at the 2007 European Union Studies Association (EUSA) Conference, Montreal, May 17–19, 2007. As of November 30, 2017:
http://aei.pitt.edu/7798/1/diez-t-01a.pdf

Dobbins, James, *Foreign Service: Five Decades on the Frontlines of American Diplomacy*, Washington, D.C.: Brookings Institution Press, 2017.

Dragneva, Rilka, "The Legal and Institutional Dimensions of The Eurasian Customs Union," in Rilka Dragneva and Kataryna Wolczuk, eds., *Eurasian Economic Integration: Law, Policy and Politics*, Cheltenham: Edward Elgar, 2013, pp. 34–60.

Dragneva, Rilka, and Kataryna Wolczuk, "The EU-Ukraine Association Agreement and the Challenges of Inter-Regionalism," *Review of Central and East European Law*, Vol. 39, 2014, pp. 213–244.

———, "The EU And EEU: Geopolitical Problems Cannot Be Addressed by Technocratic Measures," European Leadership Network, 2015. As of November 14, 2017: http://www.europeanleadershipnetwork.org/the-eu-and-eeu-geopolitical-problems-cannot-be-addressed-by-technocratic-measures_2490.html

———, *The Eurasian Economic Union: Deals, Rules and the Exercise of Power*, London: Chatham House, 2017.

Dragneva-Lewers, Rilka, and Kataryna Wolczuk, "Trade and Geopolitics: Should the EU Engage with the Eurasian Economic Union?" *EPC Policy Brief*, April 2, 2015.

Dreger, Christian, Konstantin A. Kholodilin, Dirk Ulbricht, and Jarko Fidrmuc, "Between the Hammer and the Anvil: The Impact of Economic Sanctions and Oil Prices on Russia's Ruble," *Journal of Comparative Economics*, Vol. 44, No. 2, 2016, pp. 295–308.

Emerson, Michael, "Russia's Economic Interests and the EU's DCFTA with Ukraine," EurActiv.com, June 2014. As of November 14, 2017: http://www.euractiv.com/section/economy-jobs/opinion/russia-s-economic-interests-and-the-eu-s-dcfta-with-ukrain/

Erlanger, Steven, "Russia Warns NATO On Expanding East," *New York Times*, November 26, 1993. As of November 30, 2017: http://www.nytimes.com/1993/11/26/world/russia-warns-nato-on-expanding-east.html?mcubz=0

EU—*See* European Union.

Eurasian Economic Union, Treaty on the Eurasian Economic Union, Astana, May 29, 2014. As of November 14, 2017: http://www.wipo.int/wipolex/en/details.jsp?id=15743

European Union, Association Agreement Between the European Union and the European Atomic Energy Community and Their Member States, of the One Part, and the Republic of Moldova, of the Other Part, Brussels, June 27, 2014.

———, "EU Council Press Release: Joint Statement on EU Enlargement and EU-Russia Relations," Luxembourg, April 2004.

European Union External Action Service, "Joint Press Release by the European Union and Republic of Armenia on the Initialing of the EU-Armenia Comprehensive and Enhanced Partnership Agreement," Brussels, March 21, 2017. As of November 14, 2017: https://eeas.europa.eu/headquarters/headquarters-homepage/23120/joint-press-release-european-union-and-republic-armenia-initialling-eu-armenia-comprehensive_en

Felbermayr, G. R., R. Aichele, and J. Gröschl, *Freihandel von Lissabon nach Wladiwostok: wem nutzt, wem schadet ein eurasisches Freihandelsabkommen?* Munich: Ifo Institut, 2016.

Gaprindashvili, Paata, "How to Improve Russia-Georgia Talks?" in *Georgia and Russia: In Search of Ways for Normalization*, Tbilisi: Georgian Foundation for Strategic and International Studies, 2017, pp. 5–17.

Giumelli, Francesco, "The Redistributive Impact of Restrictive Measures on EU Members: Winners and Losers from Imposing Sanctions on Russia," *Journal of Common Market Studies*, Vol. 55, No. 5, 2017, pp. 1062–1080.

Gopnik, Adam, "Are Liberals on the Wrong Side of History?" *The New Yorker*, March 20, 2017. As of November 30, 2017: https://www.newyorker.com/magazine/2017/03/20/are-liberals-on-the-wrong-side-of-history

Gower, Jackie, "EU-Russian Relations and The Eastern Enlargement: Integration or Isolation?" *Perspectives on European Politics and Society*, Vol. 1, Issue 1, 2000, pp. 75–93.

Grishchenko, Konstantin, "Za predelami shakhmatnoi doski: pragmatichnaya povestka snya Ukrainskoi vneshnei politiki," *Zerkalo nedeli*, July 16, 2010.

Havlik, Peter, Vladimir Pereboyev, Elena Rovenskaya, Anastasia Stepanova, Jurij Kofner, and Pavel Kabat, "Challenges and Opportunities of Economic Integration Within a Wider European and Eurasian Space," *IIASA Synthesis Report*, Laxenburg: International Institute for Applied Systems Analysis, 2016.

International Center for Trade and Sustainable Development, "WTO Challenges Emerge over EU Expansion," *Bridges*, Vol. 8, No. 33, 2004.

International Republican Institute, *Public Opinion Survey Residents Surveys of Georgia*, March–April 2016a. As of November 30, 2017:
http://www.iri.org/sites/default/files/wysiwyg/georgia_2016.pdf

———, *Public Opinion Survey Residents of Ukraine*, May–June 2016b. As of November 30, 2017:
http://www.iri.org/sites/default/files/wysiwyg/2016-07-08_ukraine_poll_shows_skepticism_glimmer_of_hope.pdf

———, *Public Opinion Survey Residents Surveys of Moldova*, September 2016c. As of November 30, 2017:
http://www.iri.org/sites/default/files/wysiwyg/iri_moldova_september_2016_moldova_poll_for_review.pdf

———, *Survey of Public Opinion in Georgia*, February 22–March 8, 2017. As of November 30, 2017:
http://www.iri.org/sites/default/files/iri_poll_presentation_georgia_2017.03-general.pdf

Kennedy, John F., "Commencement Address at American University in Washington," The American Presidency Project, June 10, 1963. As of November 30, 2017:
http://www.presidency.ucsb.edu/ws/?pid=9266

Keohane, R. O., and J. S. Nye, "Power and Interdependence Revisited," *International Organization*, Vol. 41, No. 4, 1987, pp. 725–753.

Kholodilin, K. A., and A. Netsunajev, "Crimea And Punishment: The Impact of Sanctions on Russian and European Economies," DIW Discussion Paper, Vol. 1569, 2016.

Korosteleva, Elena A., "Belarus Between the European Union and the Eurasian Economic Union," ODB Brussels, 2016. As of November 30, 2017:
https://odb-office.eu/files/BNV%20Survey%20Brief%20Belarus%20eng.pdf

Korshunov, Maxim, "Mikhail Gorbachev: I Am Against All Walls," *Russia Beyond the Headlines*, October 16, 2014. As of November 29, 2017:
http://rbth.com/international/2014/10/16/mikhail_gorbachev_i_am_against_all_walls_40673.html

Kostanyan, H., and R. Giragosian, "EU-Armenian Relations: Seizing the Second Chance," *CEPS Commentary*, October 2016.

Kucera, Joshua, "U.S. Blocking NATO-CSTO Cooperation," EURASIANET.org, February 12, 2011. As of November 21, 2017:
http://www.eurasianet.org/node/62882

Langbein, J., *Transnationalization and Regulatory Change in the EU's Eastern Neighbourhood*, London: Routledge, 2015.

Libman, A., "Russian Power Politics and the Eurasian Economic Union: The Real and the Imagined," *Rising Powers Quarterly*, Vol. 2, No. 1, 2017, pp. 81–103.

Mazarr, Michael J., Miranda Priebe, Andrew Radin and Astrid Stuth Cevallos, *Understanding the Current International Order*, Santa Monica, Calif.: RAND Corporation, RR-1598-OSD, 2016. As of November 14, 2017:
https://www.rand.org/pubs/research_reports/RR1598.html

"Mogherini's Spokesperson Calls New EU-Armenia Agreement 'Ambitious,'" Mediamax.am, 2017. As of November 14, 2017:
http://www.mediamax.am/en/news/foreignpolicy/22702/

NATO—*See* North Atlantic Treaty Organization.

"NATO Disregards the CSTO Suggestions About Cooperation—Bordyuzha," *Kazpravda.kz*, April 4, 2015. As of November 21, 2017:
http://www.kazpravda.kz/news/politika/nato-ignoriruet-predlozheniya-odkb-o-sotrudnichestve--borduzha

Nikitina, Yulia, "How the CSTO Can (and Cannot) Help NATO," *PONARS Eurasia*, Policy Memo 285, September 2013. As of November 20, 2017:
http://www.ponarseurasia.org/memo/how-csto-can-and-cannot-help-nato

Nitoiu, C., "European and Eurasian Integration: Competition and Cooperation in the Post-Soviet Space," *Journal of European Integration*, Vol. 39, No. 4, 2017, pp. 469–475.

North Atlantic Treaty Organization, Areas for Pursuance of a Broad, Enhanced NATO/Russia Dialogue and, Noordwijk, May 31, 1995. As of November 29, 2017:
https://www.nato.int/DOCU/comm/49-95/c950531a.htm

———, *Study on NATO Enlargement*, Brussels, September 3, 1995. As of December 7, 2017:
https://www.nato.int/cps/en/natohq/official_texts_24733.htm

———, Founding Act on Mutual Relations, Cooperation and Security Between NATO and the Russian Federation, Paris, May 27, 1997. As of November 29, 2017:
https://www.nato.int/cps/en/natohq/official_texts_25468.htm

———, Charter on a Distinctive Partnership Between the North Atlantic Treaty Organization and Ukraine, Madrid, July 9, 1997. As of December 7, 2017:
https://www.nato.int/cps/ic/natohq/official_texts_25457.htm

———, NATO-Russia Relations: A New Quality: Declaration by Heads of State and Government of NATO Member States and the Russian Federation, Rome, May 28, 2002. As of November 29, 2017:
https://www.nato.int/cps/en/natohq/official_texts_19572.htm

———, Bucharest Summit Declaration, Bucharest, April 3, 2008. As of December 7, 2017:
https://www.nato.int/cps/ua/natohq/official_texts_8443.htm

———, "Press Conference by NATO Secretary General Anders Fogh Rasmussen with Moscow-Based Journalists," March 26, 2012. As of November 20, 2017: http://www.nato.int/cps/en/natohq/opinions_85625.htm?selectedLocale=en

Novosti-Armenia, "Armenia Is a Reliable, Time-Tested Partner in the System of Alliance Relations Among the CSTO Member-States," January 18, 2007. As of November 20, 2017:
http://www.newsarmenia.ru/exclusive/20070118/41627762.html

Official Internet Resources of the President of Russia, "European Security Treaty," November 29, 2009.

———, "Remarks at the Meeting of the Valdai International Discussion Club," October 24, 2014. As of November 20, 2017:
http://en.kremlin.ru/events/president/news/46860

———, "Remarks at the 70th Session of the UN General Assembly," September 28, 2015. As of November 20, 2017:
http://en.kremlin.ru/events/president/news/50385

———, "Remarks at the Belt and Road International Forum," May 14, 2017. As of January 7, 2018:
http://en.kremlin.ru/events/president/news/54491

O'Hanlon, Michael E., "Beyond NATO: A New Security Architecture for Eastern Europe," Brookings Institution, July 28, 2017. As of November 30, 2017:
https://www.brookings.edu/blog/order-from-chaos/2017/07/28/beyond-nato-a-new-security-architecture-for-eastern-europe/

Organization for Security and Co-operation in Europe, Conference on Security and Cooperation in Europe Final Act, Helsinki, August 1, 1975. As of December 7, 2017:
http://www.osce.org/helsinki-final-act?download=true

———, Charter of Paris for a New Europe, Paris, November 21, 1990. As of November 29, 2017:
http://www.osce.org/mc/39516?download=true

———, Stabilizing Measures for Localized Crisis Situations, Vienna, November 25, 1993. As of November 30, 2017:
http://www.osce.org/fsc/42314?download=true

———, Code of Conduct on Politico-Military Aspects of Security, Budapest, December 3, 1994. As of November 29, 2017:
http://www.osce.org/fsc/41355?download=true

———, Astana Commemorative Declaration Towards a Security Community, Astana, December 1, 2010. As of December 7, 2017:
http://www.osce.org/mc/74985

———, Vienna Document 2011: On Confidence- And Security-Building Measures, November 30, 2011. As of November 30, 2017:
http://www.osce.org/fsc/86597?download=true

———, "From Lisbon to Hamburg: Declaration on the Twentieth Anniversary of the OSCE Framework for Arms Control," Organization for Security and Co-operation in Europe Ministerial Council, Hamburg, December 9, 2016. As of November 30, 2017:
http://www.osce.org/cio/289496?download=true

OSCE—*See* Organization for Security and Co-operation in Europe.

Radio Svoboda, "Prezident Ukrainy Leonid Kuchma pidpysav zakon Pro shvidkyi dostup viisk' NATO na Ukrayins'ku teritoriyu," April 6, 2004. As of December 7, 2017:
https://www.radiosvoboda.org/a/914452.html

RBC, "Russia Negotiated with Kazakhstan and Kyrgyzstan about Sending Their Troops to Syria," June 22, 2017. As of November 20, 2017:
http://www.rbc.ru/politics/22/06/2017/594bdbe79a7947172df6e0dd

RIA Novosti, "Council of the CSTO Foreign Affairs Ministers Adopted a Declaration about Cooperation with NATO," June 4, 2012. As of November 20, 2017:
http://ria.ru/defense_safety/20120406/619406089.html

Romanoff and Juliet, dir. Peter Ustinov, Universal Studios, 1961.

Rumer, Eugene, "Russia and the West in a New Standoff," Carnegie Endowment for International Peace, June 14, 2017. As of November 30, 2017:
http://carnegieendowment.org/2017/06/14/russia-and-west-in-new-standoff-pub-71250

"Russian Allies in the CSTO Do Not Want to Fight in Syria," *Nezavisimaya Gazeta*, June 26, 2017. As of November 20, 2017:
http://www.ng.ru/world/2017-06-26/1_7015_syria.html

Sarotte, Mary Elise, "Not One Inch Eastward? Bush, Baker, Kohl, Genscher, Gorbachev, and the Origin of Russian Resentment Toward NATO Enlargement in February 1990," *Diplomatic History*, Vol. 34 No. 1, 2010, pp. 119–140.

———, "Perpetuating U.S. Preeminence: The 1990 Deals to 'Bribe the Soviets Out' and Move NATO in," *International Security*, Vol. 35, No. 1, 2010, pp. 110–113.

Söderbaum, F., P. Stålgren, and Van L. Langenhove, "The EU as a Global Actor and the Dynamics of Interregionalism: A Comparative Analysis," *Journal of European Integration*, Vol. 27, No. 3, 2005, pp. 365–380.

Sprehe, Kathleen Holzwart, "Ukraine Says 'No' to NATO," Pew Research Center, March 29, 2010. As of November 29, 2017:
http://www.pewglobal.org/2010/03/29/ukraine-says-no-to-nato/

Sztompka, Piotr, "Two Theoretical Approaches to Trust: Their Implications for the Resolution of Intergroup Conflict," in Ilai Alon and Daniel Bar-Tal, eds., *The Role of Trust in Conflict Resolution*, Cham, Switzerland: Springer, 2016, pp. 15–21.

Terekhov, Vladislav, "Ob'edinenie Germanii i problema rasshireniya NATO: chto obeshchal Zapad?" Moscow State Institute of International Relations, December 21, 2009. As of November 29, 2017:
https://mgimo.ru/about/news/experts/132057

Timofeev, Ivan, *Theses on Russia's Foreign Policy and Global Positioning (2017–2024)*, Moscow: Center for Strategic Research, June 2017.

United Nations General Assembly, Declaration on Principles of International Law Concerning Friendly Relations and Cooperation among States in Accordance with the Charter of the United Nations, New York, October 24, 1970. As of November 29, 2017:
http://www.un-documents.net/a25r2625.htm

United Nations Security Council, Memorandum on Security Assurances in Connection with Ukraine's Accession to the Treaty on the Non-Proliferation of Nuclear Weapons, New York, December 19, 1994. As of December 7, 2017:
http://www.securitycouncilreport.org/atf/cf/%7B65BFCF9B-6D27-4E9C-8CD3-CF6E4FF96FF9%7D/s_1994_1399.pdf

U.S. Trade Representative, "EU Enlargement," USTR.gov, undated. As of September 20, 2017:
https://ustr.gov/archive/World_Regions/Europe_Middle_East/Europe/EU_Enlargement/Section_Index.html

"V ODKB Ukazali na Otsutstvie Sotrudnichestva s NATO," *Voennoe Obozrenie*, April 25, 2017. As of November 20, 2017:
https://topwar.ru/114228-v-odkb-ukazali-na-otsutstvie-sotrudnichestva-s-nato.html

Van der Loo, Guillaume, "The EU's Association Agreements and DCFTAs with Ukraine, Moldova and Georgia: A Comparative Study," Center for European Policy Studies, Brussels, June 24, 2017. As of November 30, 2017:
http://www.3dcftas.eu/system/tdf/Comparitve%20GVDL%2024.6.17_final_0.pdf?file=1&type=node&id=360

Verkhovna Rada, Deklaratsiya pro derzhavnyi suverenitet Ukrayiny, Kyiv, July 10, 1990. As of December 11, 2017:
http://zakon2.rada.gov.ua/laws/show/55-12

———, Pro Zbroini Syly Ukrayiny, Kyiv, 1992. As of December 7, 2017:
http://zakon2.rada.gov.ua/laws/show/1934-12

———, Pro strategiyu Ukrayiny shchodo Orhanizatsiyi Pivnichnoatlantychnoho Dohovoru (NATO), Kyiv, May 23, 2002. As of December 7, 2017:
http://www.archives.gov.ua/International/Strategia.pdf

———, Pro zasady vnutrishn'oyi i zovnishn'oyi polityky, Kyiv, July 1, 2010. As of December 11, 2017:
http://zakon2.rada.gov.ua/laws/show/2411-17

———, Pro vnesennya zmin do deyakyh zakoniv Ukrayiny shchodo vidmovy Ukrayiny vid zdiysnennya polityky pozablokovosti, Kyiv, 2014. As of December 11, 2017:
http://zakon3.rada.gov.ua/laws/show/35-19

Vinokurov, Evgeny, Peter Balas, Michael Emerson, Peter Havlik, Vladimir Pereboyev, Elena Rovenskaya, Anastasia Stepanova, Jurij Kofner, and Pavel Kabat, "Non-Tariff Barriers and Technical Regulations," IIASA Workshop Report, Laxenburg: International Institute for Applied Systems Analysis, 2016.

Voice of America, "The CSTO Invites NATO to Cooperate," December 15, 2009. As of November 20, 2017:
https://www.golos-ameriki.ru/a/nato-odkb-2009-12-15-79319727/663825.html

World Trade Organization, "Council for Trade in Goods," November 17, 2014. As of November 14, 2017:
https://www.wto.org/english/news_e/news14_e/good_17nov14_e.htm

Zagorski, Andrei, "The Transformation of Russia-ECE Relations," in Andrei Zagorski, ed., *Russia and East Central Europe After the Cold War: A Fundamentally Transformed Relationship*, Prague: Human Rights Publishers, 2015, pp. 26–58.